Baby Girl

by

Juli L. Idleman

North Shore Publishing · Boston, MA

Copyright © 2011 by Juli L. Idleman.
All rights reserved.

Published in the United States
by North Shore Publishing, Boston, MA

This book is a work of fiction. Places, events, and situations in this story are purely fictional. Any resemblance to actual persons, living or dead, is coincidental.

No part of this book may be reproduced, stored in a retrieval system or transmitted in any form or by any means without the prior written permission of the author or the publisher, except by a reviewer who may quote brief passages in a review to be printed in a newspaper, magazine or journal.

Library of Congress Cataloguing-in-Publication data
Baby Girl by Idleman, Juli.

ISBN 978-0-578-08446-6

Printed in the United States of America
First Printing June 2011

"Quis custodiet ipsos custodes?"

- Plato

Jovi, Bryant and Ryan,
without whom this story would not have been possible

Special thanks to all *those who walked
the path of adoption with my family and me. You are
too numerous to name, but you are in my heart always.*

Terminology

Child Protective Services, CPS, the Division — The agency responsible for the investigation of claims of neglect or abuse involving children, as well as the maintenance of those children when an investigation warrants removal from their current home.

Caseworker — Individual assigned the case of a child or sibling group. The primary contact for matters concerning the assigned child(ren).

Licensing Manager — The individual in charge of investigation and certification of foster and adoptive families. The primary contact for matters concerning those families.

FSTL — A meeting in which all the individuals involved in a child's case meet to discuss progress and goals.

Guardian ad Litem — An attorney appointed to represent the child's interests while in the custody of CPS.

Staffing — When a group of individuals with an interest in a child in CPS custody meet to select from a number of potential adoptive families the one they believe to be the best match for the child. Most of

Baby Girl

the people in the staffing don't have a personal relationship with the child or the key members of the child's life, especially in the case of young children.

Grievance—The process by which a decision made by the Division can be appealed. If the first grievance is denied, one more grievance—to a higher level—is permitted before the matter is considered closed.

Prologue – Day 1

"May I speak to Mandi Williams?"

"This is she."

"Hi, Mandi. My name is Racquel Watson," the female voice introduced itself. "I'm with the Division of Family Services in Anderson County. How are you doing today?"

"I'm doing well, Racquel," Mandi answered, discreetly ducking out of the training class she was attending. "Yourself?"

"Good. Thank you for asking," Racquel responded politely. "I'm calling because we have a newborn female who needs a foster home and I see you might have an opening. She is fifteen-days-old."

"We don't currently have any children with us, so there's certainly room," Mandi replied, looking out the window of the convention center. The day was overcast, rain splattered intermittently against the glass. "Can you tell me a little of her story?"

The question was a routine one for most foster parents considering a new placement, so the caseworker was ready for it. "She was left at the police station by her father at seven-days-old. He told officers — and we have since confirmed — that the mother died of drug exposure sometime shortly after she gave birth and was released from the hospital. For the time being, her name is Baby Girl, as her father stated she was never called anything specific during the week she was in their care."

Mandi grimaced, but didn't interrupt. She turned to lean against the windows, her gaze travelling the length of the hallway outside the training room.

"The baby is now at Middlepoint Medical Center in the NICU." Racquel hesitated, adding, "They do require that you be the one to go get her—we can't pick her up and bring her to your house—so they can show you how to feed her."

Mandi's mind raced, trying to rapidly process the information the woman was telling her. *If the NICU needs to show us how to feed her, then she probably has pretty serious health issues.*

It wasn't just herself Mandi had to consider, but also any impact to her three-year-old son, Matthew, and his father, Justin Rice.

"What is the status of her dad?" Mandi asked.

In reality, as foster parents, they didn't typically care what the situation was with the biological family. If a child needed a home, they had one to share. Mandi was merely trying to give herself a few more minutes to consider any potential ramifications to what the caseworker was telling her. They would not be doing anyone, including the child, any favors by accepting a situation outside the scope of their capabilities.

"The baby's father has signed away his rights," Racquel answered. "He has stated that he doesn't believe he can care for her properly. He has time to change his mind, so reunification is still listed as part of the plan, but we haven't had any contact with him since he left the police station after signing the paperwork. He was notified we would be taking his daughter to Middlepoint, but he hasn't visited her or made any effort to check on her. We don't believe he will reappear."

Mandi absorbed what the woman was saying. *So a newborn with potentially serious health issues abandoned —*

"She's actually been ready to go home for several days but I can't find a foster home that's willing to take her," Racquel commented.

And with that, the worker said about the only sentence that could circumnavigate all the reasoning and logic Mandi was trying to analyze the question with.

At fifteen, her own mother had been killed in a car accident while the two were on a road trip. Mandi ended up in the hospital where she spent the first forty-eight hours in a drug-induced coma. Due to the severity of the collision and their distance from home, it had taken the police awhile to figure out who the teenager was and get in contact with her father. After awakening, she spent another day alone in the hospital, dealing with the worst trauma of her life — the unexpected death of her mother — as she desperately waited for any familiar, living face to walk through the door.

"Ms. Williams?"

"Of course we will take her," Mandi said automatically, without any further thought.

"Great," Racquel sounded relieved, repeating, "That's great news. Are you familiar with the hospital? Will you give them a call to see if they need you to bring or have anything special?"

"I'm familiar with it," Mandi assured her. "I will call them. Do they have my name already?"

"They will in about five minutes," Racquel told her. "I will let them know as soon as we hang up."

After ending the conversation, Mandi dialed Justin to advise him of the situation, the training class she had been engrossed in just ten minutes before long forgotten.

Baby Girl

Justin had never been particularly enthusiastic about the foster care thing, yet had gone along with it for close to two years because he knew it was important to Mandi. In truth, he had an aversion to change — even rearranging the furniture caused him to become aggravated — so news of a new child always made him a bit tense.

When he answered the phone, Mandi took a deep breath and explained everything she knew about the newborn. She ended by asking, "What do you think about her staying with us?"

"I don't think it's a good idea," Justin sighed, predictably, "but it doesn't matter. You're going to do whatever you want anyway."

He was right, though Mandi gave herself credit for at least being polite enough to go through the motions of asking. In reality, she was already walking to the car.

"The father didn't even give her a name," the head nurse, Melinda Gibbons, lamented to Mandi as they walked in the room. She motioned to the pink and red construction paper sign hanging above the baby's crib, one of five in that section of the NICU. *Abigail Rose*, it declared. "Some of the nurses felt so bad about it they decided to give her one."

Looking over at the foster mother, Melinda asked, "Any idea what they are going to call her?"

Mandi shook her head, "I'm not sure. I was only told that her legal name is Baby Girl."

Walking carefully toward the sleeping baby with porcelain skin and dark brown hair, Mandi reached out and touched her hand lightly. The little girl stirred and opened her big, brown eyes.

"Well, maybe this can be her name," Melinda suggested.

"Perhaps," Mandi responded, too distracted by the fifteen-day-old in front of her to give it any serious consideration.

Noticing the woman was more concerned with the tiny being laying before them than with a discussion of potential names, Melinda said, "You got here just in time, she's ready to be fed."

"Okay, sure," Mandi agreed, forcing her gaze from the baby to look over at the nurse. "The caseworker said you need to show me how to feed her. Does she require something special?"

"No, not at all," Melinda answered quickly, waving her hand dismissively as she moved to retrieve some formula from her station, "this one is perfectly healthy."

"She is?" Mandi asked in surprise, looking around the NICU.

What's she doing in here then?

Sensing the source of the woman's confusion, Melinda told her, "She was put in the NICU primarily because of her status, because she is alone. We wanted her to have people around if she needed anything and this area is continuously staffed. It's simply a matter of policy not to discharge a baby from this unit until the parent or guardian shows they know how to feed it, though in this case it's pretty routine. Have you ever fed a newborn?"

Nodding, Mandi responded with a smile, "It's been a couple of years, but I think I can remember."

It was still raining lightly when Melinda followed Mandi out to the SUV to make certain Baby Girl was fastened into a proper car seat, another requirement of release from the hospital. The warm, late afternoon shower felt good given the heat of the past several days.

As the nurse went to close the back passenger door, she commented to the Mandi, "I'm glad to see this precious thing isn't going to be alone any longer."

Mandi smiled and nodded, "We'll take good care of her."

"I'm sure you will."

When Mandi arrived at the house, she discovered Justin and Matthew waiting to meet her. They walked into the garage almost as soon as she pulled in.

While initially intrigued, Matthew quickly grew bored with the creature who could do little more than look at him. Justin, on the other hand, was completely enamored, as Mandi had suspected he would be. Although he reacted with hesitation to change, he had not yet failed to find common ground with each of the children they had opened their doors to.

As they were eating supper, Justin commented, "I better go get that shelf in the extra room bolted to the wall. I'm going to do that as soon as we are done."

Mandi looked at him in amusement. Bolting the shelf to the wall had been discussed many times in the past months, though neither had acted on their agreement that it was a task in need of completion. Knowing the baby's utter lack of mobility couldn't be what triggered the sudden sense of urgency, it occurred to Mandi this was his way of voicing his support and acceptance of their new addition.

That tiny girl already has this big man wrapped around her little finger.

"That's a good idea," Mandi agreed, keeping the observation to herself. She smiled as they finished their meal and Justin headed off to the garage to get the necessary tools.

"You got her picked up then," Racquel said later that evening.

Both kids had been tucked into bed thirty minutes before. Mandi was in the kitchen cleaning up from supper when the caseworker called to check on their newest ward.

"Yep," Mandi replied. "She's asleep in her room now. The hospital said she's on normal feedings, so we're going to pop in every three hours or as needed like we would for any newborn. I also made an appointment with our pediatrician for first thing next week."

"Great. Also, there is an FSTL in two weeks. Will you be able to bring Baby Girl?"

Mandi had been to FSTLs in the past and seldom missed an opportunity to attend. It is when all the individuals involved in a child's case meet to discuss progress and goals. She always insisted on taking the kids in their care rather than having a social worker or parent aide schlep them around, which a number of other foster parents preferred. For Mandi, though, it was important they have as much first hand information as possible about what was going on in their children's lives.

"Absolutely," she confirmed.

"I really hate calling her Baby Girl," Racquel added as an afterthought, "especially since it's not as if there is a biological family involved."

"It is a little awkward."

"I spoke to my supervisor before I left today. She said we can't change her name legally, but we can come up with a nickname for her. We just have to be very careful to make certain all the paperwork and everything still says Baby Girl."

"Okay, that shouldn't be a problem."

"Any idea what you would like to call her?" Racquel wondered, "I can probably come up with something, but I think it might be better to let you guys since you're the ones who will be with her every day."

A name came immediately to mind, though Mandi hesitated a bit, uncertain if it was appropriate. She and Justin had decided they were done having kids, but had once discussed what they would have named a daughter if they had one.

Jade Reyna Williams-Rice.

Nothing else came to mind.

There is no plan for a daughter in our future and this little girl needs a name, she reasoned. *It's silly to hold it back for a child who will never exist.*

"How about Jade?"

"Ooooh," Racquel gushed, "I love that! That's what it will be then: Jade."

After hanging up with the caseworker, Mandi went looking for Justin. She found him in the baby's room double checking his work on the shelf. He gave it a hard tug, looking pleased when it didn't budge. Sound asleep in her crib, the little girl was oblivious to their presence.

Mandi quietly conveyed the conversation with Racquel, including that they would refer to the new addition as Jade, though her legal name would remain Baby Girl.

"So that's what a Jade Reyna looks like," Justin commented, looking down into the crib with satisfaction. "I always wondered."

1 – Day 203

"They aren't getting that baby," Edith Scarlett stated with a resolute shake of her head, placing a stack of papers on her desk. "I want the staffing scheduled in the next month."

Her remark was in reference to the text she'd received from her colleague, Payton Gringo, as she'd pulled into the office parking lot. It stated that Edith had no room on her schedule for a staffing—the process by which a family is selected as the adoptive resource for a foster child—that needed to occur sooner rather than later.

Payton started to protest, "They already have her—"

"They aren't keeping her!" Edith interrupted insistently. She glared at the woman whose desk sat adjacent to her own.

Both women worked as attorneys for the Office of the Guardian ad Litem, an agency responsible for representing the legal interests of each child in the custody of Anderson County. Of the four people juggling their caseload, Edith had seniority, something she rarely let any of them forget.

Shaking her head in resignation, Payton took another look at Edith's schedule displayed on the screen in front of her. It was jammed full of appointments, court hearings and other staffings. "I just don't see how it will be feasible—"

"Reschedule something!" Edith snapped, "Christ, it's not rocket science, is it?! This meeting has to take place before that baby has been in their home nine months. You know the deal. Once it has, they automatically get preference as the prospective adoptive resource and it becomes much more difficult to swing the staffing in our favor."

"Edith," Payton hesitated, "even if we can find a way to schedule it, their record with this child and each one before is impeccable."

Laughing conspiratorially, Edith corrected her, "Nobody's record is perfect."

"Theirs seems—"

Holding up her hand, Edith explained impatiently, "You aren't getting it, Payton. All it takes is a suggestion. The Division turns over employees so fast due to long hours and inadequate pay that everyone in that staffing will have under two years experience, all practically fresh out of college, I guarantee it.

"Also, I heard their licensing manager is out for surgery for the next six weeks. That's the person who knows them best, is likely to be their most vigorous advocate and, consequently, our largest hurdle. In her absence it is unlikely anyone there will know them well enough to have one hundred percent confidence in their competency or character. The mere intimation of something amiss will have everyone in that room second guessing what the papers in front of them say. They will scramble to select an alternative rather than risk a mistake."

Payton looked down at her keyboard. She didn't understand the reason for Edith's contempt, but the woman was powerful. She had been with the Guardian ad Litem's office for a long time. She had a strong aversion to the Children's Division, as well as to any healthy child being placed in anything less than a traditionally defined family. Traditional meaning two married parents of the same race and opposite sex, child of the same race, and a Christian religion.

Edith is entitled to her personal beliefs, of course, but her personal beliefs overlook two significant issues. First, it is against the law for her to bring them into this legal practice. Second, many of the children under our watch don't have the luxury of waiting for a family matching her ideals. They simply need a stable, loving home.

People had complained about Edith's questionable tactics before, but no one seemed able to stop her once she got on one of her missions. It bothered Payton, but she didn't need the trouble of confronting her.

It will be unfortunate for this family, but that doesn't mean the girl won't still end up in a decent home. Perhaps it will be with strangers, but she will get to know them and probably love them just as much.

Sensing her coworker vacillating, Edith hissed adamantly, "They aren't good enough, Payton. Who do they think they are trying to adopt this little girl when they aren't even married? When they obviously don't have their own moral affairs in order or subscribe to any traditional social code? Who knows what will be in store for this child if we don't intervene? They are an affront to every sound principle out there. We have an ethical obligation to intercede."

"They have been with each other for over six years," Payton responded, glancing down at the file on her desk, trying to sound matter-of-fact rather than confrontational. As much as she didn't want to start a battle with the tall, middle-aged woman whose face seemed to be perpetually contorted into a scowl, it also occurred to her that perhaps Edith simply did not have all the information on the family. She continued, "They have a little boy together. He just turned four. They have an extraordinary record with the Division. Financially, they are well ahead of most people twice their age—"

"They aren't good enough, Payton!" Edith interrupted again, obstinately, her voice rising, her face reddening.

Silence fell between the two.

Sighing in defeat, Payton finally asked, "What if the staffing doesn't go their way and they decide to fight?"

"They won't," Edith asserted with a dismissive wave of her hand. She sat down at her desk, continuing confidently. "There's no way they can. It's cost prohibitive, to begin with."

"They make good mon—"

"They won't," Edith cut her off sharply, exasperated. "Even if they are tempted to entertain the idea, everyone will dissuade them, telling them it's crazy, that they have no options, no feasible path to success. I can guarantee every major adoption attorney in this and surrounding counties will balk at taking on the Division since most enjoy the steady income from completing their uncontested adoptions. They won't want to risk making enemies. Even if they are foolish enough to move forward despite all the recommendations not to, they are almost certain to lose.

"Trust me, Payton. By the time I'm done, even they will doubt whether or not they have any right to her. Think about it. How many families have we determined were unfit? And how many have fought?"

Payton didn't say anything.

"Don't you remember that one woman?" Edith continued encouraged by her colleague's silence, "What was her name… Karen?"

"Kassie," Payton answered soberly, "and, yes, I do remember."

Edith nodded with satisfaction, turning to her computer, "Well, then, there you go. It will be just like that. We have an opportunity to do something good for this girl just as we did for that other baby."

Juli L. Idleman

Kassie Reynolds had been a foster parent for over five years. She was a single mother who entered the world of fostering when the mother of her nine-year-old daughter's best friend was about to lose custody of her kids for substance abuse. She became a foster parent, took the two girls in and eventually adopted them. Through great personal sacrifice, she saved those kids from a much more difficult life... also continuing on to foster more than thirty additional children. Everyone at the Division loved her.

They used to love her anyway.

One day Kassie received a call that the estranged mother of the two girls had given birth to a baby boy. As it would be the girls' half-brother, she was the first placement call the Division made. It was a matter of policy to at least attempt to keep siblings together. They wanted to know if she would consider taking the newest addition.

Kassie agreed, realizing she couldn't possibly tell those girls their biological brother wasn't welcome. It was a stretch on many levels, but she made it work just as any family dealing with an unexpected pregnancy might.

With the mother having disappeared once again, Kassie walked into the baby boy's staffing expecting zero opposition. He had been in their home for the previous seven months and everything was going well. There was no reason to believe it wouldn't be an open-and-close staffing... until she met Edith.

From Edith's perspective, it was simple: the boy could not go to a family whose sole provider was a single mother, regardless of the circumstances. As the staffing convened, she started talking about the possibility of drug and alcohol abuse, anger issues, suggestions of negative information heard from seemingly credible sources. Of course, all "sources" were conveniently absent from the staffing and therefore unable to confirm or deny the legitimacy of the statements. It was all unsubstantiated, but that proved irrelevant.

Edith knew what she was doing, Payton thought grimly. *It was enough. Nobody needed proof. The presumption of guilt and the burden to prove innocence landed squarely on Kassie.*

Unfortunately, as Edith also anticipated, Kassie couldn't immediately afford the legal defense or various tests to disprove the accusations. When she was finally able to scrape together the money to hire an attorney and get a comprehensive drug test done — the latter of which proved Edith's information had been completely erroneous — it was too late.

Kassie ended up with significant debt, not to mention the emotional strain on her and the girls. Despite her efforts, the baby was adopted by people ninety miles north who wanted no connection with the baby's biological family, including his sisters. It wasn't necessarily that the adoptive family was bad or to blame, it just seemed obvious to most they weren't the right family for the situation. To Edith, however, it did not matter as long as it was any family except one whose matriarch was single with three children. To Edith, it went in the victory column.

Payton glanced over at her colleague, now resolutely typing, eyes fixed firmly on the screen in front of her.

There had been complaints about how Edith handled that case and many others, but she was always able to talk her way out of it. A person could get away with a lot by claiming to only be looking out for a child's best interest.

Who would dare argue with that? Isn't that what we are all doing?

There seemed no one willing or able to quantify what 'best interest' really meant.

Sensing she was being watched, Edith asked, "Did you figure out a date?"

"I think you have time three weeks from tomorrow," Payton answered automatically.

"Perfect," she replied, pleased, having had confidence Payton would eventually come around. "Schedule it and make certain I have the names of everyone who will be in attendance. I'll start talking to them next week. It saves time if I can plant the seeds of doubt before we ever walk in the room. Might even have a few hours for the spa that afternoon," she cackled.

Payton's stomach turned, but she scheduled the meeting and proceeded to put the distasteful incident out of her mind.

Leslie Franklin was a large woman who had been with the Division most of her career. She lumbered into the meeting with Edith filled with dread.

Nobody wants this assignment, least of all me, she thought with disdain, hoisting her bag onto the table at the edge of the room with a huff.

A working group to improve relations between Child Protective Services and the Office of the Guardian ad Litem. What a waste of time.

"Leslie, I presume," a voice asked briskly.

Looking up, she found herself greeted by a scowling middle-aged woman clutching a briefcase.

Edith Scarlett. Great.

Leslie nodded, careful to keep her expression neutral changing her expression.

Taking a seat, Edith started brusquely, "You are no doubt as inspired by this assignment as I am."

Baby Girl

It took Leslie a second to read the woman, but then—recognizing the intentional sarcasm—she laughed, instantly grateful for the comradery.

"Thrilled," she rolled her eyes.

"I am going to tell you bluntly, Leslie," Edith went on in a serious tone, "that the main problem our office has with your agency is the number of things that seem to fall through the cracks, the policies that aren't quite upheld, and the records that get lost. As you are no doubt aware, these things can make our already difficult jobs even more so. I don't know what we need to discuss, as it's really rectifying those tendencies that will ultimately improve the relationship between our two groups."

"We do have a shortage of people for the number of cases we handle, an ambitious director who has reorganized and restructured more times that we can count," Leslie conceded, "but there have been improvements."

Edith was unimpressed and didn't bother trying to hide that fact, "It's not enough. We aren't there yet, not even close."

"I know," Leslie replied meekly.

2 – Day 238

The staffing for Baby Girl was well attended.

On one side of the large, square conference table were four licensing managers representing five prospective adoptive families. Among them was Lauren Sampson, acting as Mandi and Justin's licensing manager due to the fact their regular licensing manager was on leave for surgery. She had met them for the first time the week before.

Sitting directly across from the licensing managers were Dawn Cobbler, Baby Girl's new caseworker—Racquel had abruptly quit a few weeks earlier—and her supervisor, Beverly Sanchez.

At the end of the table was the adoption worker, Natalie Mills. She was in charge of implementing the findings of the staffing. Linda Niemen, from the nurse case manager's office and in charge of Baby Girl's medical records, sat next to her. Beside them was a foster parent representative, Sabrina Gable. Leslie Franklin, an administrator for the Division, was to her left. Mandi and Justin sat at the remaining side of the table, Jade sound asleep in a car seat carrier next to them.

At the last minute, Edith Scarlett from the Office of the Guardian ad Litem slid in beside Beverly, directly to Mandi's left. Mandi had never met her, but her pinched facial expression and stiff demeanor caught the foster mother's attention from the moment she joined them.

Looking around the room, Mandi counted eleven people besides her and Justin. Of them all, only Dawn had ever had any individual interaction with Jade. Of them all, only Dawn, Beverly and Lauren had ever seen Jade before this moment. Of them all, only Dawn and Lauren had ever been to their house.

Natalie opened the meeting with introductions, then prompted, "Mandi and Justin are here in their capacity as foster parents, to provide us an update on Baby Girl. They are also one of the families interested in adopting Baby Girl. Do any of you have questions for them before we excuse them, as prospective adoptive families aren't permitted to be in attendance during our deliberation?"

"I do," Edith spoke up briskly. She turned to the couple, forcing a tight smile, "I spoke to Lauren a few days ago about some questions I have. She claimed not to know the answers, as she is only filling in for your full-time licensing manager during her absence. If you don't mind, I am going to ask you those questions now."

"Sure," Mandi replied as both she and Justin nodded.

"First, you two aren't married, are you?"

They shook their heads in confirmation.

"Why is that? Do you plan to make a commitment to each other at some point in the future?"

"We feel that we already have," Mandi replied. "Justin and I have never held the belief a piece of paper was necessary to legitimize that. We feel our commitment to each other, our kids and our home speaks for itself.

"Is it an issue? We were told it wouldn't be as far as adopting Jade because there's no state law which says two people have to be married in order to adopt."

"It is an issue," Edith snapped, her face turning crimson. "Most commissioners simply won't allow it."

"How can that be if the law doesn't prohibit it?" Mandi asked in sincere confusion, her heart sinking, dread settling in the pit of her stomach.

Affronted by the question, Edith shot back, "It just is."

Mandi didn't know how to respond. She had obviously somehow offended the woman, which was the very last thing she had intended or wanted to do.

Edith saved Mandi the trouble of trying to figure out what to say in response when she continued pointedly, "And there's typically no sense in us selecting a family the commissioner is unlikely to support. It's a waste of everyone's time."

Shifting uneasily in her chair, Mandi waited for Edith to continue. She felt herself withdrawing from the confrontational nature of the woman, even though she knew there had never been an instance when it was more crucially important that she not.

Stay here.

Mandi was particularly sensitive to the hostility of others, especially when they were operating from a position of authority. It took her back to her own childhood, but not in the same pleasant way hot chocolate and Christmas cookies did. If she couldn't flee—and in this situation she certainly couldn't—she tended to pull back, her thoughts becoming difficult to articulate.

She tried to push past it, to stop the gnawing sense of doom edging into her consciousness, to ignore the part of her mind whispering that their worst fears about this meeting might already be a reality.

"Something else," Edith added, flipping briefly through some

Baby Girl

papers before leveling her gaze back on Mandi, "your mother died when you were young?"

"That's right," Mandi shifted uncomfortably once again. This woman was not one with whom it felt natural to open up to about anything personal, much less an event so devastating.

"How do you feel you did handling that?"

"I did the best I could," Mandi responded almost automatically. It was one of the first questions most people asked when they heard about the car accident that had taken her mother's life. "I was fortunate to have a strong support system that—"

"It says in your home study you were put on Zoloft after she was killed?" Edith interrupted her without changing expressions. Her voice seemed to simultaneously convey both a question and a complete lack of interest in whatever the answer might be.

"I—" Mandi hesitated, caught off guard by the inquiry.

Is this lady about to suggest...? No. Surely not.

"Yes, I was," Mandi replied, pushing her thoughts aside.

"I guess you didn't handle it as well as you claim," Edith commented condescendingly, turning to the next page.

Take aback by the comment, Mandi sputtered, surprised by the implication that somehow she wasn't being forthcoming, "I was fifteen."

Edith stared at her blankly, making it clear she felt the observation irrelevant.

"That was half my lifetime ago," Mandi continued, recovering slightly, a short, disbelieving laugh escaping her lips. "Nobody knew how I would react and the doctor suggested it to my father as a precaut—"

"You don't have to defend yourself to me, Ms. Williams," Edith cut her off with a smirk, pleased with the level of discomfort the subject had evoked. "I just need you to be honest about your capabilities when it comes to handling life events."

"Well, sure I do," Mandi answered, with a strained smiled—*Am I overreacting? Am I reading this woman wrong?*—, "you're the ones judging who Jade's adoptive parents will be, so your opinion is very important."

The others laughed.

"No, we aren't," Edith retorted quickly, vigorously shaking her head, not wanting to encourage the atmosphere of the room to lighten. "The commissioner makes that decision, not us."

"Right," Mandi agreed, trying to get Edith to relax, to realize Mandi intended no offense or harm, "but your decision certainly helps us get to that point."

"It's not up to us," Edith repeated, her anger increasing.

Mandi couldn't figure out what was going on. She couldn't bring herself to look at Justin, but could read his body language well enough to sense he was also baffled by the unexpected anger. They had not taken for granted they would be the automatic choice as Jade's adoptive resource, but they hadn't expected the hostility they were encountering either.

We didn't expect Edith.

There seemed to be more to her line of questioning than Mandi could guess, but she had a growing sense of apprehension in the pit of her stomach. No one else was asking questions, simply deferring to the middle-aged woman who seemed so personally offended.

By us? But why?

When Mandi didn't respond, Edith continued, "Your home study also says you went to see a psychiatrist six years ago. Where was that at?"

It took Mandi a moment to remember, but she nodded, "I only went once or twice, I—"

"Where was that at?" Edith asked again, rolling her eyes as if she felt Mandi was being intentionally obtuse.

"I don't recall the name," Mandi answered honestly, attempting to smile affably at her inability to remember. "It was a place out east, um—" She struggled, but it didn't come to her, "my insurance company recommended it, but I don't know. It's been so long ago. You should be able to find it in the home study. Our licensing manager requested the records from that visit during the process of licensing us as foster parents."

"Were you prescribed any medication?"

"They didn't send me to the right place—"

"Ms. Williams," Edith tried again, seeming disproportionately put out by their conversation, "were you prescribed any medication?"

"Yes."

"Are you still taking it?"

"No. I didn't take it."

"You refused to take it," Edith raised her eyebrows, nodding and jotting down some information on the legal pad in front of her.

"No," Mandi corrected her, "it wasn't what I went there for. I asked to—"

"Were you committed," the woman interrupted seriously, "or did you go there voluntary?"

"I'm sorry, what?" Mandi asked in surprise.

"Were you committed?" Edith asked shortly, "Did someone have to pick you up and take you? Was it a hospital stay?"

Mandi laughed out loud, the question striking her as absurd.

Realizing that Edith was sincerely waiting for an answer, she said, "It was voluntary. I just wanted someone to talk to because a friend of mine had been killed in a car accident similar to my mother's and I was concerned it would stir up old feelings, old memories. The insurance company sent me to a psychiatrist though and I told her—"

"Have you been back since then?"

"In the past six years?" Mandi asked pointedly. She was frustrated, though it was an emotion swiftly being overshadowed by a growing sense of trepidation. "No."

As if the foster mother hadn't said anything of relevance, Edith pressed, "And the only other time was when you were medicated as a teenager?"

"When my mother died, that's correct," Mandi confirmed dully.

She was on automatic pilot by then, despite her attempts to prevent it. She understood the woman before them was running her own agenda, had already made up her mind on their candidacy before walking in and wasn't really interested in figuring out if any of her conclusions matched reality. Or perhaps, knowing they didn't, she was just trying to prevent anyone else in the room from realizing.

Unable to determine what exactly they were dealing with, what had so thoroughly provoked Edith, Mandi could feel herself helplessly shrinking back behind her walls. Once she knew someone wasn't listening, had already made up their mind, had intentions she couldn't comprehend—any and all of the above—it was almost impossible for her to engage on any meaningful level.

"Have you been keeping Baby Girl current on her immunizations?"

"Yes," Mandi answered immediately, relieved by the simplicity of the question.

Edith appeared surprised, "Her state insurance doesn't show any record of them occurring. The state has never been charged for them."

"We pay cash so she can go to our pediatrician. Dr. Gates. He isn't covered by state insurance," Mandi explained. She glanced in the general direction of Linda, adding, "The nurse case manager has copies of all her medical records, including immunizations."

Linda didn't move or acknowledge the statement, only looked down at her hands, which struck Mandi as odd. She didn't have time to dwell on it though.

Instead of asking for proof or addressing Linda, Edith remained focused on Mandi, asking, "How many foster children have you had?"

"Six, including Jade," Justin spoke up.

Edith wasn't willing to engage with Justin, instead keeping her eyes locked on Mandi. "How many of them were removed from your care?"

"None," she replied.

"Every child went back to their family?"

"Yes, with the exception of a little boy named Brett. He kept trying to injure our dog and no one could give us anything else to try with him. That was very hard, we—"

"That's all I have," Edith interrupted. "You three can go. We have quite a bit of discussion ahead of us."

In their everyday lives, neither Mandi nor Justin were considered timid individuals, but both knew they were currently being confronted by something they couldn't entirely fathom. Without that missing piece of the puzzle, they felt powerless to address the evident tone of the room for fear of inadvertently making whatever the situation or implication was worse. They didn't know exactly what was going on, but were smart enough to realize anger and indignation would not be to their benefit.

More than a little disoriented, they stood to leave. Justin reached for Jade's car seat. She had barely stirred through the entire meeting, as it had occurred during the time of her normal morning nap.

"One last thing," Edith added abruptly, as an afterthought, "who told you it was okay to name her?"

"Her first caseworker," Mandi responded, aware this was a sore point for some. She watched as Edith seemed to shoot a pointed glance at Leslie. Mandi added hastily, "But we always make it clear that her legal name is Baby Girl."

"That's fine," Edith said shortly, though it seemed apparent it wasn't. "I'm sure your licensing manager will call once we've reached a decision."

"I just don't understand why you are so upset," Justin finally said after Jade had been loaded into the SUV and they had both settled into the front.

Behind the steering wheel, Mandi was sobbing, near hysterical.

This is bad. This is so bad.

She looked over at Justin, eyes red, "How do you not see how terrible that went?"

"I mean, I don't think it went great—I don't understand what that one woman was so unhappy about—" Justin responded, "but nothing came up that should outweigh how well Jade is doing with us. Everything she brought up, you answered."

He doesn't get it... but why should he?

It was Mandi who dealt with CPS most extensively. It had always been that way. The one thing she knew—the thing that had caused her to worry well before anyone else, well before the people never or seldom exposed to the Division or any government agency—is that logic isn't always relevant.

Yes, we did show up to give "Baby Girl" a home before knowing she was a healthy newborn.

Yes, we did run to her religiously every three hours, day or night, to feed her those first four months of her life as faithfully as we did for Matthew.

Yes, she has developed into a happy, easygoing infant who has never known a day of need or neglect out of proportion with her young life.

Yes, she has spent holidays and vacations getting to know not only us but an entire circle of aunts, uncles, cousins, grandparents, and friends.

Yes, Justin and Matthew and I, along with our extended family and friends are the only people Jade has ever known. A family she loves and who loves her.

Yes, Yes, Yes.

Mandi was silent as she navigated the vehicle back toward the house. She wanted Justin to be right. She wanted the sinking feeling in the pit of her stomach to go away. She would be more than happy to spend the rest of their lives laughing about how silly she had been to get so upset.

Mandi's heart ached. *It's not going to be enough.*

Having taken the day off from work, Mandi found herself sitting in an early movie not paying attention to anything that was happening on screen. Justin was interviewing for a new position with his job at noon so he'd had to go prepare for that. Telling herself there would be no news before one or two that afternoon, Mandi had hoped the movie would keep her from going stir crazy.

Instead, her thoughts kept returning to Edith. She seemed—through her words, her demeanor, her impatience—to have taken personal offense to something about their family.

Searching for reassurance, Mandi wondered, *Is there any way I might be reading the encounter incorrectly? Is Justin right? Perhaps I am being overly sensitive given the enormity, the stress, of the meeting?*

With the movie playing forgotten in the background, Mandi tried to understand what had happened to cause this individual to come to such an unenthusiastic conclusion about them well before—it seemed—the meeting even convened. Try as she might, she couldn't figure it out.

Thinking about it at this point is futile. Whatever it is that so rubbed her the wrong way, it is too late to go back and correct now.

Looking at the screen in front of her, Mandi struggled to blink back the fresh tears burning her eyes, to swallow against the desperate ache in her throat.

About fifteen minutes passed before Mandi looked down at her phone again. She was surprised to see several missed calls and a new text message from Justin. One call was from a number Mandi recognized as Lauren's.

Have they decided already?

They hadn't believed there would be any news this soon. Without moving from her seat, Mandi tapped on the new text message from Justin:

> **Justin Rice:** We didn't get Jade! I don't know what to—
> Sent: 11:17AM

Her heart sank. Her vision blurred. What was most amazing about that moment, however, was that Mandi managed to jump up from her seat and rush out of the theater... even as everything inside of her was collapsing.

3 – Day 238

"You were told not to get attached," Lauren Sampson said, sounding uncomfortable.

How could that even have been possible?

Mandi knew she would never forget the long walk out of the theater into the lobby where she was now standing. She had stopped there because it was raining, pouring down rain. The sky had opened up while she was in the movie.

It seems a fitting tribute.

The woman on the other end of the line continued hesitantly, "We can set up an appointment right now to get all this ironed out so when the next baby comes along, you'll be all ready to go."

What? The next…

"Lauren," Mandi stated fervently into her phone, trying to keep her mind on the task at hand rather than losing herself to the panic ripping at her heart, "we didn't get into this to adopt. We weren't and aren't looking for any random baby. We got into this to be foster parents. It just so happens one of those foster children ended up being someone we want to adopt. It wasn't a goal. No other baby can take the place of Jade. We want Jade."

"I know. Of course not," Lauren responded hastily. "I'm sorry things didn't turn out the way you hoped."

"Can you at least tell me what reasons were given?" Mandi asked. There was no way she was going to wait for some appointment several days or weeks in the future to find out what the justification had been for selecting a different family.

Lauren sighed, having hoped to put off a lengthy conversation on the subject. "Well, they just ended up deciding the Nelsons are the more suitable adoptive resource for Baby Girl."

"Okay," Mandi managed to respond, sounding much calmer than she felt, "but why is that? Jade has been with us for eight months. That's hardly insignificant. There must have been some rationale given as to why that was determined to be irrelevant."

"One reason they gave is that they thought, when you explained why the little boy who was moved… what was his name again?"

"Brett."

"Right," she continued, "they felt as if your reason for why he was moved showed that you two chose your dog — an animal — over a child who needed you."

Shocked by the assertion, Mandi felt fresh tears of confusion and frustration stinging her eyes. She struggled to keep her voice even. "We didn't choose anything over anyone. As I stated during the meeting, we didn't know how to help Brett and no one at CPS could offer us any ideas for figuring it out, so we did what we felt was best for everyone, including Brett.

"What if he had accidentally gone so far as to permanently injure or kill the dog? Would that experience have been in his best interest? We were heartbroken when he left. We tried every alternative we could think of. I was in tears the morning I had to say good-bye. You can ask our daycare."

"I'm sure," Lauren commiserated, "it just didn't come across that way to them I guess." She paused for a moment, then added, "Something else they brought up about Brett is that I guess there was a hotline about spanking involving him."

Bewildered out of her sorrow for a moment, Mandi asked in surprise, "A hotline for spanking involving who?"

"The hotline was that you spanked Brett," Lauren clarified.

What the... ?

Mandi's mind scrambled back over the three months Brett had stayed with them, now almost ten months prior. They had never heard anything but praise for the time each of their foster children had spent with them and he had been no exception.

Have I forgotten something? Some incident?

No way.

Brett was as timid as a mouse, having come from a severely abusive home. All one had to do was raise their voice and he was completely distraught. He wanted so desperately to please. There would never have been any reason to—

"Lauren, we have never spanked any foster child in our care," Mandi said bluntly. She felt some measure of hope—*if there has been a misunderstanding, then all we have to do is clear it up*—explaining, "He wasn't... I mean, when I think of some of the wild children we've had... Brett was very docile. We actually spent quite a bit of time trying to get him to assert himself because we thought that might help with whatever was causing him to be aggressive with the dog.

"We figured his behavior had to do with everything he was holding in. If he had ever felt secure enough to really misbehave, I imagine we would have been thrilled." Mandi paused, then pointed out, "Besides all that, we never heard about any hotline. Wouldn't we have been told?"

"I know," Lauren responded. "Yes, you would have been. Or should have been. I guess it was reported nine or ten months ago. We never got an actual notice of any complaint."

If there really was a hotline, why wouldn't they have followed up simply by virtue of the fact there were still foster children in our home?

Mandi wasn't certain what to say, but she pushed, "If it wasn't significant enough to mention or file an actual statement, then how can it be enough to prevent us from being selected as the resource for a child currently doing well in our care? If it is central to why we weren't chosen, then how come it wasn't mentioned while we were still in the room this morning? Why weren't we at least told so we could have had an opportunity to refute the claim?

"It's not true, Lauren," Mandi finished adamantly, "and there were more than a handful of children in our home at the time who can attest to that. It's not a legitimate reason for taking Jade."

"I know," she answered again, this time with a sigh. "I told them neither of you knew about it and it shouldn't be held against you."

"I don't understand any of this," Mandi said, the trace of hope fading, feeling utterly lost, tears starting to spill down her cheeks again.

Is this really it? Have we really lost Jade?

Mandi was still standing in front of the theater, held at bay by the torrential rain. More than one passerby had glanced at her red, tear-streaked face curiously, but she barely noticed, much less cared.

Instead of acknowledging the statement, Lauren continued, "Another factor is that when Edith asked you about your mother, she didn't feel as if you were completely forthcoming."

What?

"She asked me about my mother's death," Mandi responded, confused. "I feel as if I answered that to the best of my ability. As you may be aware, opening up about such a significant life event is very difficult. She was also pretty short, Lauren, and she interrupted every response that was more than a few words. She didn't seem very interested in detailed answers.

"Surely there isn't some suggestion I was trying to hide something? I don't dwell on the bad stuff, but instead prefer to consider the good that has come out of or despite it. That's one of my best traits. If she wanted more specific information, she could have asked more specific questions... or even have let me finish answering the ones she did ask."

"Yeah, I don't know how big of a factor that really was," Lauren confessed diffidently, wanting the discussion to be over. "It's just something she brought up so I figured I would mention it."

"Okay," Mandi replied, taking a deep breath to steady her nerves, mentally steeling herself to hear the rest. "What else was there?"

"Nothing. That was it."

Mandi didn't know what to say. She cried. A lot, in fact, for someone not prone to that particular display of emotion. Part of her knew something wasn't right—*this can't be enough to justify removing Jade from the only family she's ever known*—but the tidal wave of fear, sadness, and doubt were at the forefront, unable to be ignored much longer.

Five months before—when Jade was barely three months old—, Mandi and Justin had taken adoption classes, as required by the Division. Even then, she had been concerned about what they would do if the staffing didn't go their way and had specifically asked the instructor what options a family not selected has. They were told there was an option, although it was seldom successful at changing anything.

"I need to know how to file a grievance," Mandi said.

Lauren sighed, "I will have my secretary send you the forms."

Mandi couldn't bring herself to do much of anything after the morning they'd had. Work certainly wasn't an option, as this was a rare situation from which even that could not distract her. Instead she went home, sat on the couch in the living room and allowed herself to contemplate the enormity of what they had just endured and were about to endure.

Did we miss something? All these months we thought we were doing so well by Jade have we really been wrong? Did the people in that room see something obviously defective about our family that we somehow aren't capable of seeing?

A day without Jade in our lives? Is such a reality possible? More importantly, is it even survivable?

There had been many lows to the past twelve hours, but Mandi decided the worst part of it all had been Justin.

While she had exercised wary restraint in the weeks and moments leading up to the staffing, he had been as excited as a little kid on Christmas morning. Though they weren't supposed to present themselves as anything more than Jade's foster parents at the staffing, Mandi couldn't help but remember his introduction that morning. He hadn't been able to stop himself from declaring with a barely repressed giddiness how much they hoped to adopt the baby who was the subject of the meeting, the one asleep right beside them.

He is such a proud father, clearly doting on his daughter. Of course it would never occur to him there might be people in this world who would begrudge him that love.

Thinking of it now — of the subsequent shattered look on his face when they met up briefly after talking to Lauren, once the staffing result was known, his red eyes, his absolute distress, his broken heart — made Mandi's chest and throat physically ache.

As high as he'd been is as far as he fell.

Mandi knew she would give anything to never see anyone she loved hurt like that again. She felt contempt for the people who had been in that room. They weren't good enough to have ever sat in front of him, much less to deliver the kind of blow they did. That people so much less than him had taken a degree of peace, of innocence, of faith from him was painful in a way Mandi had never before experienced.

What kind of devastation and uncertainty have I opened my family up to by putting them at the mercy of these people – these strangers – who lack not only the time but the desire to figure out if our family is really so awful it warrants disrupting Jade's life? Have I foolishly led the people I love to slaughter? Left them to the mercy of fools?

He doesn't deserve this. **Mandi felt sick.** *We don't deserve this.*

"Ms. Williams, this is Jack Keller," the man introduced himself over the phone later in the afternoon. "I believe you left me a voicemail this morning about an adoption."

Jack Keller was an attorney well known by the Division, as well as by most foster and adoptive families. He was a frequent guest speaker at the trainings mandated for families serving in Anderson County and was, therefore, the first one most thought of when seeking legal counsel.

"Yes, Mr. Keller," Mandi acknowledged, pulling into the parking lot of her bank, the next stop on her list of errands. Beyond the windshield, the rain was still coming down steadily. "I know you do quite a few speaking engagements for CPS, so you probably don't remember us, but we are foster parents who were in an adoption class you took part in about five months ago."

After a slight pause, he admitted with a self-deprecating chuckle, "You're right, I'm afraid. I simply can't keep track of the majority of people I meet at those things. I will say," he continued good-naturedly, "that if you didn't stand out to me, that's probably a positive thing."

Mandi laughed politely, going on to explain, "Well, our situation is that we have a little girl who has been with us since she was fifteen-days-old. She is now over eight-months-old and there was a staffing for her this morning."

Taking a deep breath, Mandi tried to slow her speech despite her rapidly formulating thoughts. She tended to speak quickly at times—especially when she had a lot of information to convey—and she knew it was occasionally hard for people who weren't used to it to keep up.

"Congratulations!" Jack answered enthusiastically, mistaking her pause for the conclusion of a thought.

"No," Mandi corrected hastily, soberly. "No, we weren't the ones selected."

His voice fell, "Oh..."

"Right," she said, her eyes starting to burn again. She looked down at the steering wheel, telling him, "We are very surprised, devastated really, by the outcome."

"Did you ask them the basis for the decision?"

"We did," she answered, going on to quickly recap her conversation with Lauren.

"Huh," he said when she finished. "I'm sure sorry to hear that, but I guess I'm confused about why you called me, Ms. Williams. If not to file an adoption petition, then what are you hoping I can do for you?"

Swallowing past the lump in her throat, looking out the windshield into the water drenched world, she answered, "Besides the hotline, which—I realize you don't know us, but—that simply didn't happen, there is nothing in the reasons given that seems to justify taking Jade away. Nothing. It wasn't listed as a factor, but we believe the real reason behind the finding has to do with our not being married."

"That could certainly be the case," he agreed, "but you'll never get anyone to admit it if it is. There is nothing in the law that prohibits adoption by unmarried individuals."

"I am aware of that," Mandi told him, "because we asked everyone we encountered during the past eight months if our not being married would be an issue with this adoption. We were assured it would not be for that very reason; that there is no law preventing it."

Jack Keller had been around a long time. He was good friends with several people at the Division, with a few at the Office of the Guardian ad Litem and with some of the most well-established foster families in the county. Mandi and Justin were new to him, but there was something familiar about the story he was hearing. It seemed as if he'd heard it being discussed by some colleagues the week before.

"Mr. Keller," Mandi prompted when the man on the other end of the line fell silent, "is there nothing we can do to fight this? It's not right. Jade is happy and healthy in our care. I don't see anything here that justifies taking that away from her."

"You can file a grievance," he stated matter-of-factly. "That's the official process for appealing a decision by Child Protective Services. I can tell you that it is less than a one-percent chance it will change anything, however it will at least slow down the other couple in their attempts to adopt the child. In other words, it will buy you time, if you honestly believe time will make a difference."

"I am supposed to be receiving the grievance forms via email at some point this afternoon," Mandi told him.

"It won't change anything," he repeated, feeling obligated to help keep her expectations reasonable. "You'll get a meeting with some people in charge down there; they'll most likely uphold the findings of the staffing. You can then appeal one level higher, where they'll also likely uphold the findings. But it can be a good delay tactic."

"Okay," Mandi replied. "What else can we do though? Isn't there something that can be done on a legal level? I know the county has custody of her, but it can't be irrelevant that we have been her family for the past eight months, practically her entire life. If the staffing had happened just two weeks from today, in fact, she would have been with us nine months, giving us automatic preference as her adoptive resource."

This is the family I heard about, Jack realized. If he remembered correctly, Edith had taken a particular disliking to these two. According to her, although he couldn't remember the explanation, the couple was unfit to care for the little girl in their home on a permanent basis.

"There are certainly things that can be done," Jack responded slowly. "You can still go ahead and file an adoption petition, for one, which will force the matter before the commissioner. He'll then have to choose whichever family he thinks is the best fit."

"I see," Mandi acknowledged, grabbing a pen from her console and scribbling 'adoption petition' on a piece of paper she pulled from her glove compartment.

"To undertake something like that," he went on to warn, "would be a very costly fight—tens of thousands of dollars—and your odds of success are almost nil. It is very unlikely the commissioner will go against the Division on something like this. Has the other family had contact with the little girl?"

"No," Mandi answered, shaking her head into the phone, "that's another thing. They don't even know her. I mean, I'm sure they are probably good people and maybe she would do fine there, but why risk it when she's already doing so well with us? Everyone who visits our home or spends time with Jade... nothing more needs to be said. She's happy and she's thriving. She already has a home and a family."

"I will tell you," he hesitated for a moment, uncertain how much to reveal, "that I am fairly confident I overheard this case being discussed last week by some colleagues, individuals who were going to be in the staffing this morning. The consensus on the foster family was simply that they weren't good enough. That's what they said, in fact—that you aren't good enough."

Mandi didn't know how to respond.

If the people he overheard were talking about our family, then it means the outcome of the staffing was decided before any of us ever walked in that room. A fact which would explain why it hadn't taken nearly as long as Justin and I expected for them to reach a decision... and perhaps why no one except Edith felt the need to ask any questions.

Her mind kicked into overdrive.

Then what is the point of a staffing? What was the point of putting us through all that? Making us jump through all those hoops, explaining ourselves? Was it all just for show?

"It does sound as if you were handed a very raw deal on this one," Jack went on when Mandi didn't say anything, "but this baby was placed with your family as a foster child. You knew there was no guarantee she would end up staying. You fulfilled a role in her life—a very valuable role—and you have every reason to be proud of that. They tell you in all of your training not to get attached to these kids, yet you obviously did. You were warned not to allow that to happen.

"In a lot of ways you're really the only ones to blame for the fact today was so painful. You brought this on by believing your role in this baby's life is more enduring than it was obviously meant to be."

You were told not to get attached.

Mandi's mind almost imploded at hearing this a second time in less than twelve hours. She answered the accusation, trying to control the shaking of her voice, trying to keep her tone even, "Jade's situation hasn't been like most foster children, Mr. Keller. The biological family has never been involved, had visitation or tried to regain custody. She has had *no one* except us since the day she entered care.

"It's all fine and good in the textbook to say not to get attached, but her life started eight months ago. She couldn't wait for some silly staffing. She needed a family, people who cared enough to run into her room to feed her in the middle of the night, to love her and to protect her. That's what we did." Mandi shook her head, continuing, "If there's a way to do that without getting attached, then I will be the first to admit we don't know what it is."

Despite the strength of her words, Mandi's voice shook with disappointment and sorrow. She hated that she couldn't manage these emotions better. They would seem to recede, only to come crashing back down on her when she least expected them, when she most needed to convey her thoughts in a logical and concise manner. She wanted to have a factual conversation with this man, to sound calm and in control. He didn't know them and she felt it was imperative that he understand they were competent, devoted parents, not a ball of messy emotions... though the latter currently felt more accurate.

"It sounds as if you have loved her well," he acknowledged soberly, "but perhaps it's time for you to accept that the best way to love her moving forward might be to let her go. You have no right to that little girl. Don't be selfish. There is a process for a reason. You need to realize and trust in that."

For what seemed the hundredth time today, fresh tears began to fall down Mandi's cheeks.

Is he right? Were the people at the staffing right? Are we being selfish wanting so desperately for Jade to stay?

She looked out the driver's side window, at all the individuals passing by as if this were any other day.

"You can't win this one, Ms. Williams," Jack told her flatly, with finality. "The best you can do is help her transition smoothly to the next family. She is and only ever has been your foster child. She clearly wasn't meant to be anything more or the staffing would have turned out differently."

After hanging up with Mandi, Jack sat back in his chair, looking up at the ceiling in his office for a long moment.

Sighing, he reached for the phone on his desk. He had decided early in his career that it would be beneficial never to be on the wrong side of Edith's wrath, but he had also known it was only a matter of time before some fool would try it.

I may have just spoken to one of those fools.

"Hello?"

"Edith, Jack Keller here." Knowing that Edith wasn't one for exchanging pleasantries, he dove in, "I just had an interesting conversation about the staffing you attended this morning. It was with the foster mother, the Williams woman — Mandi Williams."

"What did she want?" Edith asked in annoyance.

"They are looking for adoption attorneys," he informed her, "planning to file a grievance."

"They weren't selected."

"She mentioned that, hence the grievance," Jack replied. "I don't believe they intend to let that dissuade them."

"They have no chance," she said dismissively, "it's a suicide mission. In the unlikelihood of a successful grievance, all it will do is go to another staffing, at which point I'll be waiting for them again. They won't fare any better in court either, though I don't blame you for taking their money if they are in such a big hurry to be relieved of it."

"I'm not planning to take the case," Jack corrected her. "It sounds like a waste of time, I agree. I trust you have done due course and if you feel they aren't up to the task of raising the little girl then they likely aren't."

"Definitely not," she remarked dryly.

"I felt kind of bad for her though," he confessed. "Can tell they are taking it pretty hard. I tried to talk her out of pursuing things further."

"Well, you did what you could, you warned them," Edith responded with a sniff of contempt. "Everything from here on out they have brought on themselves."

"Yeah," Jack faltered, "anyway, I just wanted to give you a heads up. I don't think they're going away."

Kelsey Carson chewed on her lower lip thoughtfully. She looked out her office window at the street below. On the other end of the phone Mandi was sobbing hysterically, trying to relay the story of the adoption meeting earlier that day.

This is heartbreaking.

She'd had no doubt the staffing would find in favor of her friends of ten years. *No doubt.* There was simply no explanation that made comprehensible how anyone had failed to recognize the significance of Justin and Mandi in Jade's life, not to mention the extended family, friends and community the child was already a part of. Kelsey was struggling to find the right words to comfort and encourage her friend while grappling with the nonsensical nature of the news herself.

Rubbing her eyes, wishing the rain would stop, she returned her focus to the conversation.

"I don't know, you know," Mandi was saying, sounding tired. "Maybe they are right. Maybe it is selfish to continue, to try to fight this."

"How is it selfish?" Kelsey asked with indignation, stunned by the statement.

With a sigh of resignation, Mandi conveyed Justin's devastation, the potential risk to their son and to Jade, the pessimism of the attorney she had spoken with.

"Say we fight, Kelsey," she continued, "and say we lose. I've already... If we lose her today it will be horrific, devastating... but fighting it could take months, half a year, maybe more... just to be told no all over again, to have her taken away. In the meantime, Matthew's getting older, Jade's getting older, we're all getting more attached despite the fact everyone seems to think we should be able to control or prevent that. So, you know, maybe it is selfish to hold on when there is such a slim chance it will change anything. Maybe not accepting this now will only succeed in hurting everyone—including Jade—even worse in the end."

After a short pause, during which they each struggled to understand the implications of this new reality, of the challenges ahead, it was Kelsey who spoke first.

"Fight, Mandi," she said earnestly, fiercely, with complete conviction. When her friend didn't respond right away, she persisted, "I get what you're saying and why you are saying it—it's been a long, terrible day—, but I know you. I know Justin. You have to fight. If you feel the staffing was in error, that there has been an injustice to your family or to Jade—as you obviously do—, then you will have no peace at the end of this road if you don't at least try to find the answers you need.

"They are wrong," Kelsey concluded adamantly, shaking her head and turning from the window to look out across the office. She said fervently, "Mandi. Listen to me. *They are wrong*. Underneath your grief and confusion, you know that. Give yourselves a day or two if you need, but don't let them get away with this."

4 – Day 243

"I tell you what, man," Justin shook his head. "I feel like they're trying to take my daughter."

"Well, they are."

"Yeah," Justin gave a short laugh, "yeah." He paused, "It's just that if it was anyone else, I would know what to do, how to defend my child. I would do anything—but this, the government—I don't know how to handle it, what I'm supposed to do."

Frank Randolph nodded empathetically. He was a good old boy who had retired from the same company Justin currently worked at the year before, after thirty years of service. Matthew and Jade also attended the daycare center owned by his wife, Deanna. He had run into Justin in the soda aisle of the local grocery store and—having heard the outcome of the staffing—conveyed his apologies, offering any support they might need.

What Justin needed most at that moment was a person, one not quite so close to it all as Mandi, to simply listen. As it turned out, Frank and Deanna had been foster parents when they were younger, making Frank quite possibly one of the few men really equipped to understand and meet Justin at the point he was at in his struggles.

"I just feel so helpless," Justin went on with a frustrated shrug. "I hate it. I can't protect my family. I feel as if we're being punished when we haven't even done anything wrong. These people deal with truly, truly terrible families, you know? We have watched them give shitty parent after shitty parent every chance in the world, sending kids back to homes full of abuse and drugs. What's so bad about us that they can justify such a bogus decision? I don't get it." He shook his head angrily, "I just don't get it."

"All it takes is one bad caseworker or licensing manager or lawyer," Frank agreed grimly, "and you're hosed. Everyone down there is overworked, worried about covering their own asses. More than once, Deanna and I went from being the most celebrated foster parents to, almost overnight it seemed, on our own fighting to remind those people that we were on the same side as them. We finally had to stop. The stress it was causing us, Deanna in particular... It was too much."

"That's exactly what it's like," Justin exclaimed with a dismayed laugh. "I am just so pissed. I want to beat the crap out of someone, you know?"

Frank laughed, "I know, I know."

"Except, of course, I realize that wouldn't help anything," Justin admitted with a sheepish grin, "quite the opposite. It would make me feel better though."

"How's it been going with the family anyway? I know Jade's still too young, but does Matthew have any idea what's going on?"

Justin shook his head, "Not really. I mean, I'm sure he's picked up on some sadness and tension, but he doesn't really get that Jade is any different than him. She just showed up one day as a baby, which is about how I think he figures he landed with us as well."

Frank laughed.

Baby Girl

Justin went on, "We don't want him worrying that she might disappear one day. I don't believe he would be able to comprehend that very well at this point, not without a lot of unnecessary worry."

"Sure."

"Hanging out with the kids mostly helps remind us why we're doing this, but—" With another short laugh, Justin confided, "I have to tell you… the night of the staffing we happened to have tickets to see a kids' show, a Disney show. Live theatre. We had been talking about it for weeks. Mandi and I even commented to each other that it would turn into a celebration if the staffing went well. Matthew was really looking forward to it—we were as well, truth be told—, so we decided to still go even when the celebration obviously wasn't going to materialize."

"Oh, no," Frank grimaced, remembering how shell-shocked the teachers at the daycare center had described the two as being when they picked the kids up the evening of the staffing.

"Right," Justin laughed with sincerity this time. "It was terrible. Mandi and I were sitting there like two trauma victims, trying to hold it together for the kids, too distracted to pay attention or laugh at anything that was happening in front of us. The colors seemed too bright, the characters' voices too irritating, the crowd too loud, everything too close. We did our best, but we had to leave at intermission."

"Did the kids realize?"

Justin shook his head, smiling sadly, "No, they just thought it was over, so that helped. That's the nice thing about them being so young during all this. We bought Matthew a plastic sword on the way out and Jade a fancy light-up toy and they were happy. But, man… I doubt I'll ever be able to look at a bumbling Mickey or Goofy without having horrific flashbacks."

"I hear you." Frank laughed, commiserating, "Try to keep your sense of humor though, man. It's about all you can do to prevent yourself from going crazy."

Sam Kendal leaned back from reviewing the documents in front of him. He was sitting at the end of a long conference table. Mandi and Justin, sitting directly across from each other, were to his left and to his right, respectively. They watched him consider their situation, anxious to hear his thoughts, concerned he might still tell them it was hopeless.

He was the seventh attorney they had spoken to in three days. Of them all, he was one of only two open to the idea of challenging the outcome of the staffing. The other had deferred to Kendal — declaring him the man they needed — upon hearing of his willingness to meet with them.

"I would say you have a better than fifty-percent chance of coming out of this thing victorious," Sam finally started carefully. "Now, whether that's fifty-one percent or something much better, I can't know at this juncture. We are only in the beginning stages. Your major advantage at this point is that Jade is still in your home, with your family. The longer that remains the case, the harder it becomes for the commissioner to justify moving her."

Not wanting to interrupt, the two simply nodded their understanding.

"Presuming there are no skeletons in the closets which I am as yet unaware of, and if things have happened as you indicate," he reached forward to lift one of the documents from the table, glancing over it briefly, " — which it seems as if they likely have — , then you have certainly fallen victim to an imperfect process. I would like to say that instances such as yours are rare, but unfortunately they aren't.

"In particular, you mentioned an Edith Scarlett..."

They both nodded again with Mandi adding, "She was the one who seemed most at odds with us, which was confusing and unnerving at the time. We had never met her before and she had never met Jade, yet seemed..." Mandi shook her head, at a loss for the proper description.

"She seemed angry," Justin finished, his brow furrowed in confusion, in aggravation, "and really impatient, particularly with some of the things she was throwing out at Mandi. She wouldn't even let her completely answer anything she asked."

"Well," Sam replied, "I can tell you we get a lot of business thanks to Edith." He paused, then added thoughtfully in an attempt to lighten the mood, "In fact, I really ought to send her a giant gift basket some time as an expression of my gratitude for all the work she drives our way."

Justin and Mandi laughed. It was a bit of a relief for them to consider that perhaps there had been nothing personal in Edith's attack. It meant she likely lacked the credibility they had previously granted her.

"Seriously," Sam continued, becoming a bit more sober, "as I said, I would like to tell you that your case is a rarity—and certainly in many ways it is—but the fact is this kind of stuff happens more than most people realize.

"The Division," he went on to explain, "and some of the people it employs, are in the habit of conducting themselves as if they are above the law on these matters, though it is the law itself that defines their authority. Whether it's backroom deals or politics or simply personal disagreement, certain individuals sometimes behave in a manner that exemplifies their personal beliefs and objectives, with complete disregard for legal boundaries or the best interests of the child."

After a pause, he felt compelled to remind them, "There are also, of course, plenty of extremely good people down there as well. Unfortunately, their efforts often get lost due to some of their more duplicitous colleagues."

"But how do they get away with this kind of stuff?" Justin asked in frustration, "I mean none of what's happened makes sense to me. Mandi tried to warn me, but I admit I couldn't believe…"

He paused to collect his thoughts, then continued, "I admit, as well as Jade is doing with us and as capable as we have proven ourselves at providing for her every need, I never really thought any outcome except success was possible. I never expected us to end up here." Justin shook his head, adding, "No offense," as a distracted afterthought.

Sam smiled sympathetically, assuring him, "None taken." He looked at Mandi, wondering if there was something he wasn't being told, "So you saw this coming?"

Shaking her head, Mandi explained, "I'm just the one who has interacted most with the state throughout our time as foster parents, going to the status meetings and meeting with caseworkers and all of that. I've heard stories in some of the classes they make us take. I hoped I was being overly paranoid, but I was aware that what seems like common sense to many of us often fails to translate that way when the rubber meets the road, so to speak.

"I didn't *know* there would be problems—I did wonder about the marriage issue, but every time we asked we were told it was immaterial in light of our relationship and obvious commitment to our children—but I also didn't trust that it would be as straightforward as it seemed it should be."

She paused for a moment before adding, "Then, unfortunately, the staffing happened and I knew almost from the moment Edith opened her mouth that my fears were about to be realized."

Sam nodded, taking it all in. His gut told him both Mandi and Justin were genuine in their intentions, as well as their confusion. Child Protective Services had sometimes been audacious in the pursuit of its version of reality, but this case seemed different. That they would go after a family with the credentials of this one seemed particularly astonishing, unexpectedly careless.

There has to be more to this, he thought. For the time being, however, he stuck with his instincts which told him the 'more' wasn't an issue with the two people sitting in front of him, but something beyond their blame or control.

"To answer your question, Justin," Sam finally said, "a lot of this stuff is perpetuated because many foster families simply defer to whatever CPS says. Of course, that's what the Division wants. Most foster parents either don't realize they can fight, don't care enough to try or simply can't afford it. Many rely on their foster care placements as a source of income—"

Mandi laughed in surprise. All of their foster children had always cost them more than any check that had ever arrived in the mail. It was something they were happy to do, but a money-making opportunity it was not.

"—and don't want to risk making anyone at the Division angry. Rest assured, you aren't going to be making any friends at the downtown office with this particular course of action. You may never have another foster child placed with you again.

"There are even a number of adoption lawyers who won't touch this kind of case for similar reasons. They rely on doing adoptions for Child Protective Services as a steady source of income. They don't want to land on its bad side either. It's a government agency with money to spend and, while its purpose might be more altruistic than most, don't let that fool you. It's still as marred by bureaucracy as any government agency."

Grimacing, Mandi spoke up, "We ran into that with the first several attorneys we spoke with. They weren't just unwilling to represent us in a bid against the Division, they also strongly discouraged us from pursuing it with anyone. We were told there was simply nothing to be done. You would have thought we were living under an authoritarian government the way they put things."

Sam nodded, telling them, "Usually it's a different caliber of foster parent that ends up in our office. As I mentioned, a lot of foster parents are timid and simply accept whatever the Division throws their way. The ones who end up here, who get this far, are typically made of tougher stuff. You should be proud of yourselves that you made it this far, that you didn't let anyone detour or threaten you into submission.

"That said, I don't want to mislead you... this process can be heart-wrenching for even the most put together of people."

The trio was interrupted by a knock at the conference room door. They turned just as a friendly-looking woman poked her head in, saying, "I have the documents ready to be signed."

Sam pushed back from the table, "Excellent. Come in." Turning back to the couple, he introduced the woman, "This is Samantha Moore, my paralegal. While I will be the one standing next to you in court and handling most major negotiations, she will take care of everything behind the scenes, including writing motions, making sure they get filed and, as we get further along and it becomes necessary, scheduling our court appearances."

The three exchanged greetings.

Settling into the chair to Justin's right, Samantha opened the manila folder in front of her, pulling out several pieces of paper. The adoption petition, the most significant of them all, was on top.

"I need you to read this very carefully," Sam explained as Samantha slid a copy in front of each of them. "This is what we are planning to file with the court. It will make official your desire to adopt Jade. I want you to make certain we have your names and information correct, as well as, on the last page, the name you want your daughter to have when the adoption is granted."

That he spoke as if the latter would happen made Mandi feel better than she had in days, though she knew there were still no guarantees. She scanned the last paragraph of the document.

> WHEREFORE, petitioners pray this Court that a Decree of Adoption be entered herein, providing that from the date thereof, said minor child be, to all intents and purposes, the child of petitioners, that the rights of the biological parents be terminated, that the name of said minor child be changed to Jade Reyna Williams-Rice and for such other Orders as this Court may deem just and proper.

Although they had decided the very first night that the newborn in their home would be called Jade, they had never seen the name in print in any official capacity. Everything related to their daughter, including her birth certificate, still had her as first name, Baby, middle name, Girl.

Mandi finished reading the petition, signed it and sat back while Justin signed his name. A second later, it was done.

She and Justin had been so completely devastated just days ago that—for a moment—they had lost their ability to see up from down, left from right. They had sat, utterly devastated, two normally confident, independent people suddenly held together by little more than the platinum thread of love for their children; as well as the determination and strength of friends and family who were quick to remind them who they were as they stumbled under the unexpected weight.

Though the two of them were here now, they were still trying to ramp up, to recover, to find the footing necessary to fight the very agency that had applauded and certified them as foster and adoptive parents years before. They were still struggling to wrap their minds around all the possibilities and risks now at their doorstep. The potential that their dreams of having Jade as a permanent member of their family might not be realized and what a devastating blow that would be to them, their son and those closest to them was an unbearably sobering reality. The two felt simultaneously torn between waging a war and, in the event of casualties, building a net to prevent themselves and their children from being completely destroyed.

Sam, however, did not suffer from their shock or disillusion. To the contrary, he appeared not only capable but primed for whatever fight lay ahead.

As Samantha stood and collected the paperwork, he told them, "She's going to get these filed with the court this afternoon. As we discussed, the Division isn't going to be happy you went this route. No matter what their reaction, I would recommend you continue to play it cool and cooperative. You seem like smart people, so I gather you know that, but I can't stress it enough."

Justin and Mandi nodded in agreement.

"I would like to hear what their reaction is if anything gets expressed to you. If things get contentious or they make a move to grant the other family visitation, we may have to file a motion asking the commissioner refrain from that or moving Jade until the adoption determination is made."

The thought of someone from CPS picking Jade up from daycare and giving her to the Nelsons' without notice was horrifying to Mandi. Without revealing her fears, she nodded calmly again, along with Justin.

"I will get these filed," Samantha reiterated, moving toward the door. Addressing Mandi and Justin, she said, "I'm sure we'll be speaking in the days ahead."

"Thank you, Samantha," Sam answered. "Let me know if you need anything more from me to get this done."

As Samantha left the room, Sam turned to the couple, saying almost apologetically, "I will tell you that, while I know this isn't what you wanted things to come to, it's cases like yours that make my job interesting. A lot of the simpler, straightforward adoptions we don't even touch anymore because they are just boring. We let the other attorneys have those. However, when cases such as yours come my way, that's when I'm reminded why I got into this field to begin with."

Mandi didn't resent the man for his enthusiasm. She had a feeling, in the weeks and months ahead, when words were lost on them, it would make him their best advocate.

The weeks and months ahead.

She had many questions about what those weeks and months would bring... and a hard time not yet having the answers.

Win or lose, what Mandi and Justin ultimately wanted Jade to recognize — whether by them telling her or through some obscure legal document discovered in a future they weren't permitted to be part of — was that she had not been given up twice. Her biological father's inability or unwillingness to fight had not been mimicked by the family that had cared for her since the day she left the hospital.

Mandi hoped that, no matter what, if their daughter ever looked back at these days, she would see there had been people who had known she was worth fighting for.

"Thank you for holding. My name is Emily Warren, identification number 2-3-9-0-8," a female voice came over the line. "How may I help you today?"

"I would like to disconnect our cable service," Mandi said, leaning back in her desk chair.

"Okay, ma'am, I can help you with that. May I ask why you are choosing to leave us? Is there a concern I might be able to help you address?"

"No," Mandi answered sincerely, "our family just has different priorities right now."

"It appears you've been a loyal customer for eight years. Are you certain there is nothing I can do to change your mind?"

"No, thank you," Mandi repeated firmly.

An hour later, she had completed canceling the cable service, the home phone service in favor of mobile service, the remainder of the work on the back patio, as well as a handful of other nice but unnecessary monthly expenditures. The new tires for the car would also have to wait, as well as the trip to Boston and several other places that had been tentatively planned for later in the year. Justin was going

Baby Girl

to sell the SUV and rely solely on his work truck for transportation.

Mandi reviewed the spreadsheet in front of her. It was a good start. There were other things that could be sold or cut, but they had decided to stop there until they could get a better idea of the financial impact they were looking at.

Kendal & Kendal had required a ten thousand dollar retainer. Sam also warned them they could be looking at two or three times that amount before everything was settled. Neither wanted to use credit or borrow from their savings or retirement to cover the costs, so they had set to the task of ruthlessly slashing expenses in order to redirect as much disposable income as possible to attorney fees.

Leaning back in her chair, Mandi looked at her bookshelf.

It isn't going to be easy.

It was difficult not to feel a little resentful about the inconvenience they were facing, but Mandi knew if they could scrape through the months ahead this way, at least once everything was over, the recovery would be quick. No loans to pay off, only—*hopefully*—the four of them to pick up, dust off and move forward.

There is a time for building, Mandi reminded herself, *and a time to throw everything out that doesn't matter, piling sandbags around everything that does. This is that time. The storm will pass, we just have to ride it out.*

5 – Day 247

"Where are you?" Anna Montgomery, the office manager at the kids' daycare center, demanded as Mandi brought the phone to her ear, before she could even say hello.

Surprised by the normally affable woman's tone, uncertain if she was just playing around, Mandi answered, "I'm actually pulling in the parking lot right now. I got off work early and am planning to take the kids to the nature trails."

"You need to get in here *NOW*," Anna said urgently, her voice rising, the strain more than obvious.

"What's going on?" Mandi asked, feeling suddenly panicked, knowing that Anna wasn't prone to dramatics.

She pulled into the closest parking space available, shoving the transmission into park before the car had completely stopped. It jerked to a halt. "Is everything okay? Are the kids okay?!"

"The kids are physically fine, but things are soooo not okay. Are you here?"

Jumping out of the car, Mandi jogged toward the building, "Walking in the door now."

Before she could even wave her security card in front of the scanner, the door buzzed to let her in. The site that immediately greeted her in the lobby was the owner, Deanna Randolph, and Anna squarely faced off with Dawn—who was inexplicably holding Jade—and her supervisor, Beverly. All five turned to look at Mandi.

In one swift glance, Mandi took in the aggravation etched on Deanna's face, the barely controlled outrage in Anna's furrowed brow, as well as their physical placement between the Division workers and the door. She noted the strained look on Dawn's face, the indignation of Beverly's and that Dawn didn't move to hand Jade over when the little girl reached for Mandi, eager to get away from the anxiety she could sense in the situation.

Sam said something about this possibility, part of her whispered in dismay, as she mentally scrambled to figure out what was happening.

"What's going on?" Mandi asked, trying to keep her voice calm, her breathing even, and her mind open.

Neither of the caseworkers answered the question.

"Well, tell her!" Anna exclaimed, "Christ's sake. You can't just walk in and take Jade without at least telling her!"

"Really, guys," Deanna said in disgust, "this is no way to thank the families who volunteer themselves for these children. Or, for that matter, daycares like ours who take care of those same children while the parents work. It's not our job to break this kind of news."

"What the hell is going on?" Mandi demanded, her growing panic manifesting itself as anger.

By now, Jade was straining hard against Dawn's grasp, whimpering, desperately reaching for Mandi. Dawn's eyes were firmly on the ground as if she was unaware of what the eight-month-old wanted. Before any of the women could react, Mandi quickly crossed the distance between her and Dawn, impatiently extracting Jade from the caseworker's arms.

"You can't—" Beverly started to protest, taking a step toward the mother and child.

"Tell me why I can't," Mandi shot back, meeting the woman's gaze evenly. Moving back, Jade firmly on her hip, she continued, "I walk in to what is clearly an unpleasant situation, the youngest member of the group immediately reaching to me for some sort of comfort and you're telling me that whatever is going on here has made us such barbarians I can't offer that to her?"

"We are taking Jade to the Nelsons," Dawn mumbled, looking at her shoes.

"We don't owe an explanation—" Beverly chastised her subordinate furiously.

Mandi was struck dumb for a moment, feeling as if she had just been punched in the stomach. A handful of thoughts hit her mind at once—*On whose authority? Does this make the adoption petition moot? Is this legal? Without even letting us say good-bye? What if I hadn't been early today? I would have just shown up and she would have been... Really?*—and a handful of thoughts made her mind go blank. She shook her head in disbelief, at a loss, "Wow."

"I told you that you needed to get in here," Anna spoke up, grimacing, glaring at the women in front of them.

It was the last thought that stuck with Mandi. Addressing Beverly, she asked incredulously, "You don't owe us an explanation?"

"By law, Jade is in our custody and your guardianship is only on our authority," Beverly pointed out. "We can revoke that authority at any time."

"You don't owe us an explanation?" Mandi asked again without raising her voice, truly mystified by the statement.

"You are making this harder than it has to be," Beverly

complained, rolling her eyes impatiently.

"Explanations aside," Mandi asked, her brow furrowed in confusion bordering on disgust, "what about the opportunity to say good-bye? You were seriously about to take the little girl who has been a permanent part of our lives since she was two-weeks-old and not give any of us a chance to say good-bye? To have some closure in the event—" Mandi's throat constricted at the thought, making it impossible for her to even utter the words *in the event we never see her again.*

"We have a schedule," Beverly interrupted in annoyance. "We're short staffed—"

"And yet not so short staffed that two of you couldn't be here," Deanna commented.

"It's a matter of policy when we're picking up a child to have more than one caseworker in attendance," Beverly replied shortly.

Recovering, Mandi asked, "You couldn't even call? It didn't occur to you that Justin and I might find moving her out of our home so significant an occurrence that we would miss work in order to be here?"

As her shock wore off, Mandi felt her indignation rising, "You were seriously going to let us walk in this evening and just find her gone? You really think we deserve that?"

"We were going to call once we had her picked up," Dawn protested half-heartedly.

"That's great, Dawn," Mandi retorted, as disgusted by the woman's weak demeanor as by the incident itself. "That would have been a real comforting call coming two minutes after it was too late to properly tell her good-bye or whatever it is this is supposed to be. Why is she being moved anyway?" Mandi looked back at Beverly,

"The staffing was only a little over a week ago. The commissioner hasn't even heard the case."

"CPS doesn't need to give its foster parents a reason for removing a child from their home," Beverly said again, her voice dry as if bored by a conversation she found tedious and unnecessary.

"Are you even human?!" Mandi blurted out in disgust, her temper momentarily getting the better of her, unable to comprehend the woman standing before her.

Deanna and Anna laughed at the unexpected outburst.

"Excuse me?" Beverly asked sharply, her eyebrows shooting up in surprise.

Mandi wasn't happy about the momentary loss of control—*it won't help us in the long run*—but she had a hard time not calling things like she saw them. Instead of repeating herself, she focused on stalling, "We have filed an adoption petition with the court. Jade can't be moved until the commissioner decides on the case."

"There's no reason she can't wait with the Nelsons until that judgment is made," Beverly disagreed, taking a step toward the foster mother. "They were the ones selected by the staffing, the ones the Division is choosing to support. CPS has the ability to make placement decisions until that time."

Jade buried her head in Mandi's shoulder as Mandi took a step back to counter the move by the supervisor. She pressed, "Is there some complaint against us? Some assertion that she isn't safe or doing well in our care?"

Dawn shook her head, "There's no complaint."

"Then why?" Mandi demanded again in disgust, "Why is this necessary? You're really just going to dump her on a family she has never met and yank her away from the only one she's ever known without any sort of adjustment period or anything?"

"She won't know," Beverly argued. "She's not old enough to require an adjustment period."

"Did you see that baby reach for her mama as she walked in the door?" Deanna spoke up furiously, pointing at Mandi and Jade.

"She knows exactly who her family is," Anna agreed, "and she sure as heck knows you're trying to take that away! Look at her! She doesn't want to go with you."

Beverly went on as if the two hadn't spoken, repeating, "Once a staffing occurs and a family is selected, we have the authority to move a child into their care in whatever manner is deemed best. Sometimes that's gradual visitations leading up to permanent placement, but sometimes it's just a direct placement. Given your conflict of interest in this case, your desire to adopt Baby Girl and your possible hard feelings over not being selected, simply moving her without preamble has been determined as the best route."

"We have filed a grievance to the staffing," Mandi told her, throwing out the last thing she could think of. "The staffing cannot be upheld until the grievance is settled."

Dawn and Beverly glanced at one another.

The exchange was not lost on Mandi. She felt hope desperately surge through her as she thought of the attorneys' words, *It will buy you time...*

"You know I'm right," Mandi pushed, not letting the moment pass, not giving them time to make excuses. "You aren't supposed to be doing it like this—you don't have the court's authority or even correct Division protocol, not as long as the staffing is being appealed."

"You know what," Deanna added, waving her finger at Beverly, "she's absolutely right. We were foster parents for fifteen years so I know something about this. You cannot circumnavigate a grievance."

Exasperated, angry at being cornered, Beverly said, "I'm not going to discuss CPS policy with you in the middle of a pick-up. If you have a complaint—"

"What?" Anna cut her off, "File a grievance?"

Even Mandi couldn't help the short laugh that escaped her lips at the office manager's remark.

"We came here to pick up Baby Girl," Beverly continued firmly. "We aren't leaving without her."

"Call the police," Mandi said suddenly, not completely sure what she was saying or planning, but determined there was no way she was going to just hand Jade over without knowing she had tried everything.

The mouths of the two women working for the daycare dropped, as did Dawn's, but Mandi was resolute, repeating, "The only way you are taking Jade right now is if you call the police."

"We have the clout, Ms. Williams," Beverly warned, looking at the woman with sincere curiosity, wondering what she was counting on. "They will side with us. They won't have any choice."

"Call them," Mandi said again, barely able to hear over the blood pounding in her ears.

"Honey, I don't know—" Deanna started hesitantly.

Mandi was certain. "I want there to be a record when I file my second grievance about the first grievance being ignored; and when I call the news stations; and when I show up at the state capital."

Dismissively, Beverly started, "You wouldn't—"

"How far would you go for one of your children?" Mandi snapped furiously, taking a step toward the woman she had been backing away from for the past ten minutes. She was tired of this game, tired of the supervisor's insolence. "How far to protect your family?"

Taken aback, Beverly clamped her mouth shut.

"You think you have leverage?" Mandi demanded, not backing down, Jade staring at her in wide-eyed wonder, "Your only leverage is this little girl so long as she remains under our roof. I don't know what the hell happened at that staffing, but I know the life Jade is having speaks for itself, as does our record as foster parents and as members of this community.

"And you are *grossly* underestimating me if you think you can swoop in here and callously take her without expecting a fight the likes of which you and this agency have not bargained for, lady. I will make certain the crass negligence of everyone involved, starting with you, becomes a well known fact and an interminable thorn in the side of CPS. You take Jade and see just how far I will go when there is nothing left to lose."

No one said anything for a moment.

Finally, Beverly tried a different approach, her voice taking on the tone of a patient negotiator, "Ms. Williams—"

"Call them or I will," Mandi cut her off firmly, done with the conversation, the wrangling. These were points on which she would not waver, to which there was no compromise. Pulling her phone from her back pocket, she held it out to the supervisor. "If you are certain you aren't breaking policy or law, then you have nothing to fear from anything I might do as a consequence."

Beverly didn't reach for the phone, but Mandi didn't retract it. Jade, along with the rest of the group, was watching the exchange anxiously.

Tired of the stand-off, Mandi asked, "Do you want me to call?"

"It seems—" Beverly started slowly, "It seems as if there has been a misunderstanding. Our intention was never to upset you or," she looked at the daycare center staff, "anyone. Baby Girl might not need an adjustment period, but it's obvious you do. We will let her stay with your family while we go back to the office to see if we can figure out a different approach."

"That sounds fine," Mandi said, not allowing her face to betray any emotion, though relief washed over her so quickly and completely it made her knees weak.

"We'll be in touch," Beverly said as she and Dawn made their way out the door.

Sliding her phone back into her pocket, Mandi realized she was shaking.

"Here, honey, sit down," Deanna said quickly, able to see the color draining from Mandi's face as the significance of the close call they had just had started to sink in.

Mandi sat down, looking at the two women, hugging Jade, shaking her head in disbelief, "Oh my god."

"You handled that very well," Anna assured her.

What stops them from showing up and trying this again tomorrow? Are we not going to be able to let Jade out of our sight until this is settled? Would five minutes, the decision not to leave work early today in light of the nice weather, have cost us our daughter? Is everything really so tenuous?

"Oh my god," she said, shaking her head again.

"We'll file the motion requesting that Jade not be moved until the adoption decision is made," Sam told Mandi not an hour later. "I will have Samantha do that now, then rush service to the Division so they should be served by tomorrow. It will cost extra, but—"

"That doesn't matter," Mandi assured him quickly, pressing the phone to her ear so she could hear better as she drove the kids to the trails. "Do whatever you have to."

"Can you keep Jade home from daycare tomorrow?" Sam asked, explaining, "I don't want to risk sending her back before we know CPS is aware there is a motion pending on the issue."

"No problem," she replied. "I can either work from home or take the day off; anything I need to do. I can't imagine how horrific it would have been to arrive to pick up the kids, excited for our outing, only to find her gone."

"Quite frankly, I am shocked they would be so brazen," he told her candidly. "Beverly had to know they weren't following procedure. She must have hoped you wouldn't realize or perhaps that's why she didn't give you any notice. Either way, I certainly don't understand what they were thinking, unless it's just they know they don't have a case for not selecting your family and were simply hoping to remove the primary advantage you have with her already being in your home."

"I don't know either," Mandi said. "I got lucky on the grievance thing. It just popped into my head. I didn't really think I could stop them."

Mandi was tired of talking about it, of thinking about it. After the debrief with Deanna and Anna, the play-by-play to Justin, the call to the attorney... it was all starting to feel surreal.

It was such a close call... the timing... too close.

"We're going to file the motion in the next thirty minutes." Sam said again, "Keep Jade home with you until we receive confirmation CPS has been served—it should be tomorrow—and definitely let me know if anything else comes up. For the time being, until that motion is filed, I would say you and Justin are also too busy for any home visits or anything like that over the next several days. Don't give them any opportunity. You had the advantage of surprise today. If they get a second chance, they will likely be better prepared, perhaps even showing up with the police to save you the trouble of calling them."

Mandi shuddered. *That would no doubt get ugly.*

The attorney asked, "When is your grievance meeting scheduled?"

"Next week."

"In that case, I would even hold off any contact with the Division until after that time. You should still return calls — don't give them an excuse to come looking for you — but you're too busy over the next week for any face-to-face visits. Schedule them if you have to, but set them for after the grievance hearing. You don't want to get to that meeting with the panel having become biased from hearing one-sided versions of your encounters with their workers."

"I understand," Mandi agreed wearily.

6 – Day 255

Justin and Mandi arrived at the downtown office of Child Protective Services with ten minutes to spare. They found the meeting room their letter referenced, taking a seat on the side of the narrow conference table facing the door. Within a couple of minutes, they were joined by two women.

"Are you Mandi and Justin?" the shorter of the two asked.

"Yes," they both answered, standing as the women entered.

"Great, you're right on time," the first answered as she reached for each of their hands. "My name is Cheri Wilson. We spoke on the phone, Mandi." — Mandi nodded in recognition — "and this is my supervisor, Valerie Francis. She reports directly to Vanessa Lane, who heads the entire Anderson County Child Protective Services Division."

Introductions aside, Valerie shut the door to the room. The four sat down, with Mandi and Justin retaking their original positions, Valerie and Cheri sitting directly across from them.

Cheri began, "As it was I who received your grievance letter, I am familiar to some degree with the reasons you have requested this meeting. However, for continuity, as well as to get Valerie completely up-to-speed, there might be a bit of redundancy as we get underway. Please don't conclude this to mean I wasn't paying attention during our previous discussions."

"Sure," the two agreed.

"Okay, good," Cheri nodded, looking down at the notes in front of her. "I believe this is in regard to a staffing a couple weeks ago for a foster child currently in your care. Is that correct? The specific issue being that you weren't selected as her adoptive resource and are unhappy with the outcome?"

Both nodded.

"Let's start there then," Cheri suggested. "Why do you feel the selection is in error?"

Mandi had decided to defer primarily to Justin during this conversation. She still wasn't entirely certain what had rubbed Edith — *she seemed to take genuine, personal offense to me* — the wrong way and she wasn't about to risk the same mistake with these ladies.

Starting carefully, Justin said, "We picked Jade up from the hospital when she was fifteen-days-old. In the time she has been with our family —"

"Jade is what you refer to Baby Girl as?" Valerie asked, scribbling the name on her notepad.

"Yes," Justin nodded, waiting a moment to see if she would pursue the question further. When she didn't, he continued, "In the eight months Jade has been with our family, she has developed into a carefree, playful little girl who is always quick with a smile. When she came into our care, she was in the twenty-fifth percentile for weight, height and head circumference. During her last two trips to the pediatrician, her percentiles are at fifty-five, fifty and fifty-five for weight, height and head circumference, respectively… holding steady at well above when she came into our care.

"In the past eight months, she has also started crawling, standing, babbling, had her first tooth, her first Christmas and her first trip to Disney World. As significantly, no one has ever expressed any concern about her placement with our family. In fact, most are quick to comment on how happy and well-adjusted she seems."

"Has she had the developmental assessment done yet?" Cheri asked, referring to a standard test administered to most children within the Division's custody.

Mandi, who handled most of those appointments, nodded confirming, "Last month. She was found to be on target, if not ahead of where they expected her to be."

Valerie nodded. Both she and Cheri scribbled additional notes on the notepads in front of each of them.

Uncertain whether or not he was supposed to continue, but not having been asked to stop, Justin went on, "In light of these things, the fact we weren't chosen as Jade's adoptive resource—and the reasons given for that—appear incredibly weak. Unbelievable, really."

"Okay," Cheri acknowledged, "let's talk about those things."

"Well," Mandi spoke up, "of the few reasons I heard, the two that seem most significant to me involve a little boy who was last in our care about ten months ago. We ultimately requested that he be removed from our home, after he had been with us approximately three months, due to the fact he kept trying to injure our dog. Brett was sweet and docile around people, but he was outright abusive when it came to Charlie."

Justin nodded in agreement, adding, "and we couldn't keep the two apart. Charlie got to where he would try to avoid Brett, but he couldn't all the time."

"I tried to explain the situation at the staffing for Jade," Mandi said, "but the woman asking most of the questions—"

"—all of them—" Justin corrected.

"—didn't seem very interested in detailed answers. I was told by Lauren, who was in attendance on behalf of our regular licensing manager, that my response was construed as us choosing our dog over a foster child, or biological family over a foster child, or something like that." Mandi shook her head sadly, "In truth, we really did care about that little boy. We just had no idea how to help him."

"That must have been a difficult situation for your family," Cheri remarked sympathetically.

"It was," Mandi agreed, hoping the other woman was as sincere as she was. "The other thing we heard—for the very first time—immediately following the staffing was that there had been a complaint I spanked Brett on one occasion while he was at our house."

Taking a deep breath, as she found this reason particularly disturbing, Mandi said, "I was completely taken aback when Lauren told me that. First of all, it didn't happen. As I told her, Brett was the most timid kid. He wanted to blend in to the wall more than he wanted to draw our attention for any reason, good or bad.

"Second, he came from a very abusive situation at home, then was at three different foster homes—within six months—before ours. Including his biological mother, he had no less than five individuals he called 'Mom' in one year.

"Third," Mandi grimaced, "and this is our primary objection, nobody mentioned this to us while we were at the staffing. Edith asked us all these supposedly imperative questions, but somehow failed to bring this issue up in order to at least afford us an opportunity to refute it.

"Of all the reasons we were given for not being selected as Jade's adoptive resource, this one seems most significant, so why wasn't it mentioned at any point in the ten months since it supposedly happened, much less during the twenty minutes we were sitting right in front of them?"

"You specifically mentioned this to me when we scheduled today's meeting," Cheri remarked with a nod. "I wondered the same thing myself and, as a consequence, have done a little digging since we last spoke. I went through your licensing record and through Brett's case file. I did a search related to caseworker, parent aides and all parties involved at that time. There is no record of a hotline."

"Well, that's good," Justin responded with relief that quickly turned to confusion, "but then where did the accusation come from?"

"I'm still trying to figure that out," Cheri admitted, "but even if someone did think you used corporal punishment, there was definitely no accusation of abuse or neglect, so it would simply have been reported as something against CPS policy."

It started to dawn on Mandi that it seemed as if Cheri, at least, might be as puzzled as them.

A grievance never changes anything, she reminded herself firmly.

"What were the other reasons you were given?" Valerie wondered.

"The only other thing that was mentioned to us," Mandi answered, "is that I guess Edith didn't feel I was very transparent when she asked about my mother's death. Lauren said she didn't know how big of an issue it really was, but that Edith mentioned it. I suppose if she felt I was hiding something, then maybe..." her voice trailed off as she shook her head in confusion.

"That woman was incredibly difficult to talk to," Justin spoke up grimly, "and, for some reason, she seemed to have it out for Mandi. I don't exactly understand what the deal was there, but I can't imagine what else she could have wanted Mandi to say about such a traumatic incident in her life. She would barely let her get two words out as it was."

"That's true," Mandi agreed. "She definitely didn't seem very interested in answers and it's already not a subject I open up to just anyone about."

"That's reasonable," Valerie said, pointing out, "If you did open up about it to everyone that would seem a little odd as well."

"Was there anything else?" Cheri inquired.

"No," Justin replied, "we were hoping you might know of any other reasons they had."

"I'm afraid I don't," Cheri admitted with a shake of her head. "I have the notes from the staffing here and I don't see anything mentioned other than what we have already addressed."

Part of Mandi wanted to push, to insist these women acknowledge that the findings of the staffing not only didn't make sense but were completely ridiculous. She restrained herself, instead opting to convey their theory about the motivation behind the outcome that day, "We suspect—though it wasn't brought up as a reason—we suspect that our not being married was the real issue."

Justin nodded, "As soon as the staffing began, Edith made it very clear that most commissioners won't approve an adoption to an unmarried couple. She seemed incredibly aggravated when Mandi pointed out that there is nothing in the law which says an unmarried couple can't adopt."

"That's true," Cheri responded, "there isn't. Same sex couples have adopted children and, obviously, the law doesn't currently permit them to marry. There are some commissioners who don't really approve of it, but any and all of those concerns should have been investigated and resolved during the process of your licensing as foster and adoptive parents."

Silence fell amongst the group as they each reflected on the situation.

"I can't imagine why this would be an issue," Justin brought up, trying to think of anything else that might help the women understand the situation better, "but Edith also seemed to take offense to the fact we named Jade. We made it clear to her we still legally refer to and respect her legal name of Baby Girl. Calling her something else wasn't a matter of presumption on our part, but practicality."

"Besides us, nobody in her life—daycare, caseworkers, doctor, or otherwise—, wanted to refer to her as Baby Girl," Mandi explained. "It just seemed too cold. In fact, you should have seen the looks we got from the flight attendants when we had to put Jade's plane ticket to Florida under her legal name. I pointed to Matthew and said his name was Baby Boy," she joked, "telling them we aren't very inspired people."

Justin laughed at the memory along with Cheri and Valerie.

"There's no reason that should be an issue," Cheri assured them. "In fact, I specifically remember the original caseworker asking me about it. She didn't have a name, no biological family was involved, and it wouldn't have made sense to call her Baby Girl all these months. Besides, by now, even if she is adopted by another family who names her something different, it would still be a change to her whether she thinks her name is Baby Girl or Jade."

Mandi felt herself relax. Justin seemed to sink further back into his chair as well.

"I am curious about something," Valerie started.

The three of them turned to look at the woman.

"Are you both confident that, no matter what, you can provide for your children now and in the future?"

"Absolutely," Mandi said right away.

"Without question," Justin answered at the same time.

"You believe that you have a healthy relationship?"

They each nodded.

"Well," Justin said as an afterthought, "except when she gets passive aggressive. That's never fun, but I have yet to see her direct it at the kids."

Mandi's jaw practically dropped. She was far from infallible, but doubted most would describe her direct—sometimes too much information—approach to life as passive aggressive. She waited for him to continue, hoping he knew what he was doing.

"Meaning?" Cheri asked curiously.

"For example," Justin answered, "the first level of the house has wood flooring. Do you know what she does when she gets angry with me?"

"What?" Valerie asked, her eyes wide.

"She waxes it without warning me," he told the women matter-of-factly, "then she laughs when I go crashing across the floor."

"She laughs when you hurt yourself?" Valerie asked in concern, though both she and Cheri had smiles tugging at the corners of their mouths.

"Oh, yeah," Justin raised his eyebrows, enjoying the captive audience, "hysterically even."

It took Mandi a moment to remember what he was talking about, but then she laughed out loud. She could see his eyes twinkling. He was enjoying the attention, the break in the seriousness that had pervaded the room until that moment.

"Exactly what I'm telling you," he pointed out to them, motioning disdainfully to Mandi laughing.

"It was just once a couple months ago, though he has yet to let me forget about it," Mandi explained with a grin, shaking her head dismissively. It felt good to smile despite the gravity of their current situation. "I went to clean the floor one morning, realized we were out of floor cleaner so decided to use the wood furniture polish instead because, you know, it's all wood. I'd never tried it before. It actually worked pretty well except—"

The two women groaned. "You can't do that," Valerie interrupted with a chuckle.

"Well, once I did, I realized it was pretty slippery," Mandi admitted, "but I figured if we were all careful it would be all right. Take off the socks not just the shoes when we came in, stuff like that."

"Mm-hmm," Justin commented skeptically, "yet somehow it didn't quite work out like that, now did it?"

Smiling, she continued, "I was at my desk working that evening when he got home—I had completely forgotten about the floor by then—and I heard him enter, followed almost immediately by him hollering, "*Jesus tits!*" then this loud crash as he desperately grabbed for the counter in an effort to catch himself."

The memory of his exclamation, of the *uh-oh* that crossed her mind the second she heard it, caused her to laugh hysterically as she struggled to add, "I felt really bad."

"Obviously," Justin remarked with a roll of his eyes, playing the role of victim well.

Cheri and Valerie were laughing.

"How did we get on this subject again?" Mandi finally wondered, with a shake of her head, trying to get her laughter under control, wiping at her watering eyes.

"I asked if you two believe you have a healthy relationship," Valerie reminded her.

"Oh yeah," Mandi remembered, answering, "Well, I don't know if it's normal, but I think it's pretty healthy. I have yet to land him in the hospital at least."

"I'm sure it's only a matter of time," Justin ruminated.

Smiling, Cheri said to Justin, "I appreciate you sharing the story. It certainly helped to lighten the mood a bit, as well as give us insight into your relationship."

"It did," Valerie agreed, also addressing Justin, "and you should consider yourself lucky. As my husband would be quick to tell you, I've done much worse."

Mandi and Justin laughed.

"Something else," Justin brought up, becoming solemn once again, "and I'm not sure what made me think of this, but an individual Mandi spoke with informed her that the outcome of the staffing was decided the week before it actually occurred."

Both women's eyebrows shot up, all business once again.

"Is that true?" Valerie asked, turning to Mandi inquisitively. "Who did you hear that from? Who did they say told them the staffing was decided before the appointed time?"

Mandi avoided identifying Jack Keller, but confirmed, "It is. I was told that the week before some people were overheard discussing this case, at which point it was conveyed that our family wouldn't be selected because we were simply not good enough.

"Which," Mandi went on, "if that's the case, and the decision is made in advance of the actual staffing, then I guess we wonder what the point was of forcing everyone to show up that day. It seems we suffered needlessly if there was little hope of a different outcome regardless."

"We don't know if it's true, but it would explain why they reached a decision so quickly," Justin remarked. "We expected that the process would take the better part of a day, or at least half a day, yet we had a call telling us the verdict not more than one-and-a-half to two hours after we left."

Neither Valerie nor Cheri seemed to know what to say. They simply glanced at each other, then back at the two in front of them.

"It's just really disappointing," Mandi stated with resignation and a sad shake of her head. "There's no way it's in Jade's best interest to be taken from her home. No way. I'm sure the Nelsons are probably good people, and maybe there is some life or social yardstick they measure higher on, but that doesn't make them any more Jade's parents than it makes them Matthew's. Nobody knows that little girl like we do, just like nobody knows our son like we do.

"She is so happy, so at ease. If she was having a bad life, there's no way she would be like that. I mean, I guess we can have the whole nature versus nurture debate," Mandi shrugged again regretfully, "but I don't believe she would be how she is if we were such an awful family that it really justifies uprooting her like this. I feel as if that might have been discovered had the tone of the staffing been more conversational than confrontational."

"I agree," Justin told them, "like Mandi mentioned earlier about the hotline... Why wouldn't Edith do more research before throwing something that damaging out? Or at least bring it up with us still in the room? It really seems as if they walked in there believing things that had nothing to do with who we really are, then directed the meeting in a way that would lend credibility to their preconceived notions rather than making an honest attempt to discover the truth."

Cheri pursed her lips grimly.

"You do know that Edith doesn't work for the Division, correct?" Valerie said in response, visibly agitated, though it didn't seem to be directed at them. "In fact, any complaints about her behavior should be directed to her supervisor. Her name is Margaret Brinkle."

Mandi was surprised by the information, but jotted it down on the notepad she'd almost forgotten was sitting beside her.

"Have you hired an attorney?" Cheri asked.

"We have," Mandi admitted, wondering if this wasn't already a well known fact since CPS should have been served twice by now, once for the petition, then again for the motion not to move Jade. "He filed the adoption petition a little over a week ago."

"Who is it?" she followed up, pen poised to write.

"Sam Kendal," Justin answered.

Remembering what Sam had said about how the Division wouldn't be happy to hear they'd taken the matter to court and not wanting to derail the positive tone of the meeting, Mandi explained, "We weren't certain how long it would take to get a grievance meeting scheduled and we didn't want Jade's life disrupted in the interim."

Mandi was aware she might be reading the woman wrong, but — despite Sam's warning about their displeasure — Valerie seemed visibly relieved by the information.

"The Nelsons have requested visitation," Cheri informed them with a nod.

Mandi felt her chest tighten.

"Of course," Cheri clarified, "until the grievance process is complete, we won't be able to grant that."

Justin and Mandi nodded in relief.

"Is there anything else either of you would like to add before we wrap this up?" Cheri asked.

"Just," Mandi started cautiously, still wanting to tread carefully, "I know everyone keeps telling us we weren't supposed to get attached, but we are. We have been there every step of the way with Jade and we want to continue in that role. More than just our selfish desires, though, this seems incredibly unfair to Jade.

"We are the only family with memories of picking her up from the hospital. The only family who heard the stories of her first days from the nurses, know what they named her, how they passed the time to make certain she wasn't lonely. We are the people who have seen so many of her firsts. We know her stories. I could share those things with a new family, I guess, but we are the only ones with the firsthand experience of those events, just like a biological family would have.

"It's true that she can't articulate her preference and that, if she's taken away now, she won't be able to ask for or even remember us, but I am convinced she will know. She'll know she's in a different home with different people, a different daycare with different friends. And I know — *I know* — some part of her will wonder where we've gone, why she lost *everyone* she loves. That's not right. That's not fair. Not when the reasons are as flimsy as the ones we have been given thus far.

"We came here today as ready to hear a valid explanation for this... this *tragedy* as anyone. A reason we could use to justify even to ourselves that, yes, maybe the Nelsons do make more sense, but we still don't have that. And that's..." Mandi shook her head in frustration and sorrow, "this entire situation is just very disappointing, very sad."

Valerie handed a box of tissues to Justin with a sympathetic smile.

Mandi looked over in surprise to see that his eyes were red, tears standing in them. She could tell he was trying to hold them back, but his reaction had obviously not been lost on either Valerie or Cheri.

"We do want families to get attached to the children in their home," Cheri stated kindly. "That's what most of these children need after the kind of stuff they have been through. They need parents who are going to take a vested interest in their lives and well-being. Neither of you have done anything wrong here.

"We are going to discuss what we've learned during this conversation as well as what my own research has uncovered," Cheri explained, "then take those things, along with our conclusions, to Vanessa Lane for review. You will receive a letter in the mail with our findings. We very much appreciate you taking the time to meet with us today."

Nodding, expressing their thanks, Mandi and Justin stood, moving toward the door.

Valerie opened it for them, smiling kindly. As they went to pass through, she said, "If Baby Girl—Jade—is thriving as you say, then you have obviously done quite a bit right. I hope that will bring you some degree of peace."

7 – Day 264

Edith slammed her briefcase down on the desk, causing an engrossed Payton to jump.

Looking over at her, Edith asked angrily, "Did you hear?"

"Hear what?" Payton asked in confusion.

"The Williams-Rice adoption," she snarled in response. "That cocky bitch in charge of the Children's Division, Cheri Wilson, overturned our staffing!"

Stunned, Payton didn't know what to say except, "She did?"

"Yeah," she retorted, furiously jabbing at her computer's power button. "Can you believe that?"

"So there's going to be another staffing?"

"No," she shook her head in disbelief. "No, I mean, you would think, wouldn't you? But, no, she flat out overturned it and selected them instead!"

"Unbelievable," Payton replied in awe. She shrugged her shoulders, not nearly as displeased as her colleague, "Well, I guess that's that."

"The hell it is!" Edith shot back indignantly. "We're going to throw our support behind the first family, the Nelsons. They are the right family for Baby Girl. Married fifteen years, humble, religious people who have fertility problems. They'll appreciate that baby in a way this young, self-indulgent, unmarried couple can't even begin to!"

The statement was so blatantly biased, so illegal, that Payton looked around to see if anyone else had heard it or was within earshot. As luck would have it, the desks surrounding them were empty, most of their occupants out to lunch.

She replied tentatively, "I imagine any couple who has faced infertility might appreciate a child a bit differently—not necessarily better—than one who hasn't. Yet I'm skeptical that automatically means she will be more loved or have a better life."

Edith stopped, surprised by the uncharacteristic rebuttal.

Payton waited, regretting the assertion the minute it crossed her lips, thinking, *I really don't want to deal with one of her temper tantrums right now.*

"What's up with you today?" Edith finally asked grumpily, sitting down at her desk with a huff, "I thought we were in agreement about how unfit her current foster family is to adopt her?"

"Edith," Payton sighed—*shut up, just shut up*—, "I have to be honest. I looked at the Nelsons' file, in anticipation of having to support their selection once it gets to court, and I'm not seeing it. I sincerely can't imagine what you all were thinking when you chose them."

"What is that supposed to mean? They are a perfectly respectable couple!"

"You know exactly what I mean," Payton replied grimly. "Maybe they have been married awhile, and I certainly agree that's an important fact, but it's about the only way they rank higher than the foster family, at least on paper. That might have been okay before this got overturned, but now... What do you expect me to go to court with?"

"They were the best couple of the ones we had to choose from," Edith conceded reluctantly, before obstinately adding, "but they are still a better option than this Williams-Rice family."

"What makes you think the Nelsons won't back off now that the original decision has been overturned?"

As if she had been waiting for the question, Edith leaned forward eagerly, "I heard they are planning to press forward with their adoption petition despite the Wilson woman's verdict, which is what I meant when I said we are going to throw our support behind them. They are very angry at having been de-selected without so much as being granted a meeting themselves. I don't blame them."

"That's interesting," Payton said slowly.

"Meaning?"

"It's just..." Payton hesitated, "I mean, have they even met the baby? They weren't at the staffing were they?"

"No and they haven't, but what has that got to do with anything? A family doesn't have to meet a child to be selected as its best placement. All you have to do is voice your support for the Nelsons and there's no way the commissioner will go against our recommendation."

"Well, given they've never met and have no bond with the child, and now don't even have the support of the Division, not to mention the issues I was referencing earlier," she practically whined, "I think there's every reason the commissioner might not only reject our recommendation but tell us we've lost our minds. They are effectively strangers, Edith."

"It doesn't matter. They are the more stable family."

"There's really no evidence of that," Payton pointed out, feeling anxious. "Two more weeks and the law would have automatically given the Williams-Rice family preference. They'll be well past that timeframe before this ever makes it to court."

"That's immaterial," Edith fumed, put off by the unexpected opposition from her normally passive colleague. "The nine month preference applies to the staffing, nothing after that. Otherwise every foolhardy foster family angry they weren't selected could simply drag out the adoption past the ninth month in order to bend the system to their will."

The thing Payton hated worse than the idea of a confrontation with Edith was the thought of the commissioner blasting her in court for supporting such an inexplicable selection. That potential humiliation was the only reason she was willing to risk upsetting Edith by continuing to prod.

"You really should have given me more to work with here," Payton complained with a shake of her head. "Have you even looked to see who the commissioner is on this case?"

"I haven't," Edith admitted, "that's your area. You and Steve handle the court appearances, Kristy and I handle the FSTLs and staffings. I don't want to step on any toes by doing your job."

"Well," Payton said with a sigh, the irony of Edith's statement not at all lost on her, "I have looked. It's Roberts. Does that change your mind on this?"

"Why should it?"

"He's more progressive than many of the other judges," she pointed out. "He's even granted adoptions to same-sex couples, which—as you are aware—are not able to get married in this state."

Edith rolled her eyes, disgusted by the thought, though she understood that for some children there was no other option.

When she didn't comment, Payton continued, "Also, he is himself a divorced father of two. He's not likely to put much stock in the marriage card, and if he looks too closely at the Nelsons' situation—"

"He won't look that closely," Edith rolled her eyes again, cutting the woman off, irritated by her audacity. "Progressive or not, the commissioners don't have any more time or energy than the rest of us. Full dockets, not enough hours in the day... I can assure you, he won't look that close."

"He will if the Williams-Rice attorney asks him to," Payton muttered.

"What did you say?" Edith demanded.

"Without the commendation of the Division," Payton spoke up, "the Nelsons might as well be any random couple off the street trying to adopt that girl. There are zero advantages for them or us to play up."

Exasperated by the dialogue, Edith repeated, "Figuring out how to pull it off is part of your job, Payton. Kristy and I go to the meetings, you and Steve fight to support our decisions in court."

"You seem confident," Payton said skeptically. She shook her head yet again, having second thoughts about opposing her coworker, "Look, I apologize if it seems I'm being difficult, but I really can't imagine what it is you're counting on."

"The fact is, as you mentioned, the hearing is likely a long ways off," Edith answered with a shrug.

"What's that supposed to mean?"

Smiling smugly, she confided, "Remember that silly committee I was asked to join to work on the relationship between our office and Child Protective Services?"

"No, I don't—"

"You know, the one they brought up at our last all-hands meeting," Edith reminded her. "The goal is to work on communication, resolve some of our hard feelings toward each other, blah, blah, blah..."

"Okay, sure," Payton nodded, mystified as to how one related to the other. "I do recall that."

"Well, I've struck up a sort of friendship with the representative for the Division, an overweight woman by the name of Leslie who is absolutely desperate for someone to listen to her ideas." Edith laughed, "All I do is listen and she's so grateful for someone willing to sit there while she snivels that she takes all my ideas straight back to the Division for implementation, no questions or complaints. She's practically my own personal puppet."

Payton's stomach turned. *The woman is foul.* She asked, "What has that got to do with me making a case for the Nelsons out of nothing?"

"Anyone who is at a staffing can appeal Cheri's decision," Edith said deviously.

Scrunching her forehead, Payton asked in bewilderment, "Don't you think it will start to look a little one-sided if you—"

"Not me," she cut Payton off impatiently, "Leslie. I made certain she was at that staffing just in case there was an issue. I'm going to convince her she needs to appeal it being overturned. Pretty clever, right?"

Payton remained skeptical, reminding Edith, "Cheri and Valerie are Leslie's supervisors. I don't see how you can possibly expect to convince her to go against them. That would likely be incredibly awkward for her—"

"Leave that part to me," Edith interrupted with smug confidence. "Just be prepared to throw your support behind the Nelsons when this thing gets to court. Maybe reach out to them in the meantime and encourage them to remain involved in the event they're having any doubts. Let them know we are on their side and believe their continued participation will be in the best interest of Baby Girl."

The restaurant was noisy, filled with a boisterous after work crowd. The worn out, pale complexions of both Edith and Leslie were reflected in the mirror stretching the length of the wall, their serious expressions indicative of the tense conversation they were embroiled in. Even had anyone noticed the two sitting at the bar, talking intently, it would have been nearly impossible for them to overhear the exchange due to all the noise, which is how Edith had planned it.

"That could make for a very uncomfortable situation for me," Leslie remarked apprehensively.

Edith had asked her to meet for drinks after work claiming she wanted to discuss a situation involving some of her colleagues without the risk of anyone eavesdropping.

They were each on their second drink before she broached the subject of the Williams-Rice staffing being overturned. It wasn't news to Leslie, but Edith hadn't expected it to be. She figured the entire office had been advised of the outcome in anticipation of any fallout. Leslie was shocked, however, when Edith went on to suggest that she be the one to appeal the decision.

"I totally get your concerns," Edith was saying in an atypically sympathetic tone, "but this is the kind of stuff you and I have been discussing in our meetings about how to promote better relations between our two offices."

"It is?"

"Sure it is," Edith answered sweetly, barely keeping her

impatience in check. "Turning over a staffing that contained more than a dozen individuals and a day of discussion in favor of the opinion of two women sitting in a room with that couple for a mere hour or so? It doesn't make any sense. At the very least, there should have been another staffing." She shook her head and paused to take a drink, finishing with, "To completely circumnavigate the process? It's absolutely infuriating."

"I guess so..." Leslie replied uncertainly.

She wanted Edith to like her—or at the very least to not cause trouble for her as she had for others—so she didn't point out the obvious errors in the woman's statement, such as the fact they didn't talk to Mandi or Justin for even twenty minutes before ruling them out nor did they spend a day in that staffing seriously weighing all options. Edith came in and strong-armed the entire thing, taking advantage of the fact most of them were relatively new. Which, of course, was the primary issue CPS had with the Office of the Guardian ad Litem; one that was also supposed to be getting addressed by their workgroup, though Leslie had yet to be as skillful at asserting their side as Edith was at asserting hers.

"There's no guessing so," Edith corrected, seeming to stiffen at the suggestion, at the unexpected push back.

First Payton, now Leslie... Why is everyone being so difficult today?

"Well, why can't you appeal it then?" Leslie wondered, her unease growing.

"Because," she explained, "since I was the one who did most of the questioning at the staffing, it would be too easy to make it appear as if the appeal is just about me being unhappy rather than the group."

"Isn't it?" Leslie asked without thinking. The look on Edith's face made her instantly regret the question.

"No," she shot back angrily. "Absolutely not. Everyone in that staffing voted for the Nelsons."

"Then why does it have to be me? Why can't one of them appeal the decision?"

This time Edith couldn't stop herself from ticking impatiently, "Because you are the only one brave enough to speak up. All of those other Division workers, I'm sorry to say, they just aren't up to par."

Leslie shifted her body uncomfortably on the bar stool. She appreciated the compliment, but part of her suspected Edith's purpose in saying it had more to do with personal motivation than sincerity. Her personality was meek and somewhat innocent, but that didn't mean she wasn't smart. Attempting to push the doubts aside, she tried, "It's not that I don't agree with you to some extent. I just don't want to get into any trouble."

"What trouble?" Edith asked.

"I dunno," Leslie shrugged. "I mean, Cheri does my performance review which impacts my raises. She has ultimate say on any time I take off, on whether or not I even continue to work there."

"She is legally prohibited from punishing you for appealing her decision," Edith stated matter-of-factly. "If she does anything to you in response to your appealing the staffing out of genuine concern, then you can sue her and the agency and," she chuckled, "simply retire early."

Leslie grinned half-heartedly. The words were some relief to her, but she still wasn't sure. Despite what she was saying to stall Edith, it wasn't really the idea of Cheri being malicious that she was worried about. In truth, vindication simply wasn't in the woman's nature.

It was that something felt... dirty about the entire exchange, though she couldn't quite put her finger on what it was. She was starting to get the feeling maybe Edith wasn't being truthful about her desire to mend fences with the Division but might, instead, be using her as a pawn.

Leslie wasn't certain where the thought came from but she felt guilty the moment it crossed her mind.

You've always been insecure, she chastised herself. *Edith has never been anything but gracious and receptive.*

It didn't change the fact, however, that while she may have been astonished to hear that Cheri and Valerie overturned the staffing, she had also worked with both women quite awhile and knew neither easily suffered fools. If they felt the Williams-Rice couple was better suited for the baby girl, then odds seemed good they were.

Edith took a last swallow of her drink before setting it down on the bar with finality. After all her years as an attorney, she knew when to make her case and when to back off before the other party started feeling too pressured. Even the most simple-minded of human beings typically wanted to feel they were making their own decisions, were in charge of their own destiny, rather than feeling manipulated. It didn't mean they really were, of course, they just wanted to feel that way. During her days as a criminal attorney, she had won many a jury on that principle alone.

"I have another appointment to get to," Edith said smoothly. "Give some thought to what we've discussed, if you don't mind. I will respect your decision either way, though I certainly believe it will further the work between our offices if you can help me out here. I know it will take a great deal of courage on your part, but I wouldn't ask if I didn't know you are one of the few capable of handling it."

At her words, Leslie felt doubly guilty for her reservations.

Edith stood up to leave, putting some money on the counter to cover their tab. "I've got this. I appreciate you taking the time to meet with me," she stated. "I really do enjoy working with you, Leslie. The Division needs more employees like you. Please let me know what you decide."

Surprised by the sudden retreat and the expression of appreciation, Leslie barely managed to respond, "Okay, sure," before Edith turned and disappeared out the door.

8 – Day 290

With sickening abruptness and clarity, Mandi realized they had taken her ten-month-old daughter, Jade, over a week before and weren't planning to give her back. She, Justin and Matthew hadn't seen her in close to nine days.

"They want to put her with the Nelsons for now," their attorney had told them in a placating voice. "I think it's okay if we let them. We'll get her back after the trial."

Now, more than a week later, Mandi's heart pounded.

They aren't going to give her back. If they were, then why would they have moved her to begin with? Why did we let them take her? Why didn't we realize when Sam told us the plan to hand Jade over that it didn't make any sense? Why didn't we get a second opinion, a third, a fourth? How did we miss that?

She felt sick.

We were tricked into giving up the daughter and sister we have been fighting so hard for.

Remembering the day they had met the Nelsons to let them pick up Jade, Mandi felt her stomach twist in trepidation. The memory of their beautiful little girl smiling and babbling was so clear it felt as if she was still right there…

Baby Girl

Except she isn't, because we gave her away.

Jade was with the Nelsons now and it was becoming very clear to Mandi there was no reason to believe they would ever see her again.

Jade.

Mandi was forced to think about what their family would look like without the cheerful girl they had come to love so entirely. It didn't appear anything like before she had joined them a mere ten months prior. All the emotional and financial cost fighting to adopt their daughter had now translated into a life sentence for their family, one of incomprehensible pain and heart-wrenching incompleteness.

How will we ever move past such a tremendous loss? How will we live without the enormity of this overshadowing all our moments from this day forward?

Mandi knew Jade wouldn't remember them, even though they were and always would be her family, part of who she was.

Has she already forgotten us? Does she wonder where we have gone even though she can't ask? Does she think we have abandoned her?

Desperate, Mandi reached for her smartphone and opened the browser. She had only spoken to the Nelsons once, the day they had turned Jade over to them, but she had to call. She had to try to reason with the couple, to beg that her family at least be allowed visitation.

Why didn't we think to ask for that before agreeing to let her move there until the trial? A date hasn't even been set yet. We have no way of knowing how long it will be.

Mandi had no idea what the Nelsons' phone number was, but she intended to find it.

It's been over a week, her mind whispered desperately.

Mandi woke up drenched in sweat. She had dozed off on the

couch in the living room. Sitting up slowly, she looked around, feeling ill. Her heart was pounding.

It took her a second to realize it had all been a dream.

It isn't true, she told herself firmly. *The kids – Matthew and Jade – will be home with Justin any minute. They will be home any minute.*

It isn't true. Jade is still here.

It was a relief, but it took several more minutes for her mind to get her body to accept that the intensely sick, desperate feelings hadn't been valid, weren't necessary.

Giving herself a mental shake, Mandi got up from the couch and walked to the kitchen to start preparing supper for a family gathering they were hosting later in the day. Pulling the hard-boiled eggs from the refrigerator and starting to peel them, she reflected on the events of the last few weeks.

The Nelsons are angry. There can be no mistaking that.

News the staffing had been overturned hit Justin and Mandi like warm sunshine exploding unexpectedly unobstructed through an unbearably long, cold, cloudy day. The rush of joy at the news had literally taken Mandi's breath away, an amazing feeling after weeks of struggling every time the possibility of losing their little girl crossed her mind. Finally behind them were the days of walking into daycare every evening, terrified someone would tell her the caseworker had picked Jade up and taken her to the Nelsons without even letting them say good-bye; as was the perpetual fear of being one minute too late to prevent it.

Passing on the news to their attorney, he had expressed nothing short of amazement.

"Congratulations!" he exclaimed sincerely, "You are one of the few families I know of who have had a grievance actually come out in their favor. You should be very proud of that, as it means you must have handled yourselves and the pressure of the meeting extremely well. Don't get me wrong, it does happen, but it is incredibly rare."

Unfortunately, the good news stopped there. Upon receiving notice the Division had decided to overturn its original recommendation of them as Baby Girl's adoptive resource, the Nelsons didn't disappear as everyone had hoped, but chose to persist in their fight. They had never met the ten-month-old but had become convinced it was the baby they were meant to have.

As for their own convictions, Justin and Mandi believed the Nelsons were decent, well-intentioned people who had also been dragged into an undesirable situation due to the faulty staffing. They didn't blame the other couple for their confusion, their hurt or even their anger. In a different setting and without so much at stake, Mandi might even have risked reaching out directly to Danielle Nelson to see if they could come to a mutual understanding about the circumstances.

This wasn't a normal situation, however, and the stakes were breathtakingly high. Mandi didn't know Danielle and it seemed too much to risk attempting to interact with her only to potentially have something misconstrued or taken out of context.

What if I talk to her only to have it twisted as my trying to pressure or intimidate them in some way? What if instead of seeing our side, it only makes them angrier, more determined?

She had learned it wasn't safe to assume rational was a word that applied to those involved in this fiasco. For the time being, it would have to be left to their lawyers to hash out.

Matthew interrupted Mandi's thoughts by sauntering into the kitchen as she was in the midst of peeling the last egg.

"What's goin' on, bud?" She greeted him, looking up briefly from her work, "Did you have fun with Dad?"

"Uh-huh," Matthew answered, climbing up on a stool they kept in the kitchen so the kids could reach the sink and the counter. He leaned against the cabinet next to Mandi and asked, "What'chu making?"

"Deviled eggs."

"Ew, I don't like those," he declared, scrunching up his nose.

Mandi laughed, "Yes, you do, silly boy."

"No, I don't. They are stinky yucky."

Smiling, Mandi reminded him, "Every time I make these you say—" she scrunched up her own nose, pausing her work to lean over and look him in the eye humorously, "*—Ew, I don't like those—*," Matthew giggled in response, "—but then you always want, like, *twelve*."

After watching Mandi mash egg yolks for a few seconds, Matthew informed her, "I want to be an adult."

Looking over at her son in amusement, she asked, "Oh yeah? Why is that?"

"When I'm an adult I'm going to make things too and ride big roller coasters and do whatever I want when I'm a big kid."

Mandi smiled at the repetitiveness of his declaration, but admitted, "There are certainly advantages to being an adult."

"Yeah," he said enthusiastically, "when I'm big I can drink grape soda whenever I want and stay up until midnight on not just New Years and my friends and I are going to live in airplanes."

"That sounds like a lot of fun," Mandi agreed. "Of course, there are disadvantages as well."

"Like what?" he wondered.

"Well," she thought about it for a few moments, "like having to pay for stuff. How will you get money for your adventures?"

The four-year-old giggled, "I will get it from you and Dad!"

Mandi laughed, "I don't know if it works like that once you get to be a big kid."

"You're silly, Mom," he told her dismissively, hopping down to go play with Jade.

Justin walked into the kitchen, catching the end of the conversation.

"I'm guessing there was a turf battle over the grape soda again?" she asked as their son retreated.

"I told him he had to wait. It was like the world ended." Rolling his eyes good-naturedly, Justin said pointedly, "There is only one person I know of in this world more stubborn than your son."

Mandi grinned, turning back to her work as he went to join the kids in the other room.

A few minutes later, the phone rang. Looking over at the caller ID flashing on the display, Mandi saw it was their attorney. Quickly wiping her hands off on a towel, she grabbed the device, tapped the screen and put it to her ear.

"Hello?"

"Mandi, it's Sam Kendal."

"Hey, Sam," she greeted him.

"Do you have a few minutes?"

"Sure."

"Well, so, as you are aware, the Nelsons didn't withdraw their petition as we would have liked. I still can't quite figure out what's motivating them to move forward, to be honest. Are you certain they have never met Jade?"

It was the third or fourth time he had asked the question in as many weeks. As with each time before, Mandi told him, "Pretty sure.

She has definitely never met them while with us and she is only without us at daycare. The daycare says no one from CPS has ever brought anyone by. They seldom visit themselves."

"Okay, well," Sam continued, "it's a mystery to me then why they would persist in this fight."

"I did speak to their attorney, Kelly Ceasal, today about the potential of having you and Justin meet with the Nelsons. When I probed a bit on why they might be pursuing this adoption despite not having even met Jade and no longer having the support of the Division, she seemed to indicate the possibility of some religious motivation."

Stunned, Mandi asked in confusion, "What does that mean?"

Sam hesitated, "I'm not entirely certain. She seemed to think they feel they have a spiritual obligation to your child and that is the primary motivation behind their failure to cease and desist, if you will. I guess they are very involved in their church."

Mandi wasn't sure what to say, so she didn't say anything.

"I certainly don't want to use religion against them in court," Sam continued, "as I am a religious individual myself, but if there is anything excessive there—"

Mandi couldn't help but picture Jade growing up in a dark cellar with no access to the outside world.

"—I definitely want to be aware of it. I'm going to try to find out more, but if you hear of anything along those lines, please let me know."

"Sure," she agreed.

"Another thing I was able to find out," he went on. "Were you or Justin aware that the Nelsons are on state aide?"

Shaking her head into the phone, Mandi asked, "What's that mean exactly? Like, welfare?"

"That's right," Sam confirmed. "The wife is an administrative assistant, but apparently the husband has been out of work for quite awhile."

"Are you kidding me?"

"I'm not," he responded. "Of course, income doesn't mean that these are bad people or unfit parents—"

"No, of course not," Mandi agreed hastily.

"—but when the existing family, with the established bond with the child, can better provide for its future, it further adds to the enigma of what could possibly have justified appointment of this particular family to begin with. I know for a fact Kelly is getting paid by the state, which means they even asked for assistance with their adoption fees."

Feeling frustrated, Mandi started mashing the rest of the ingredients into the yolks to give her something secondary to focus on as she remarked, "We hoped the further we got into this the more answers we would find, but instead it just makes less and less sense. There only seem to be more questions."

Sam sighed, "I know what you mean. The good news is we haven't found out anything anyone has on you that we didn't expect. What we're looking at right now just seems to be a lot of inconvenience and, unfortunately for you and Justin, money spent to remain in this battle. I am still hopeful we can prevent this from going to court contested by getting the Nelsons to agree to meet with you both prior to that. I believe if they do, it might help open their eyes a bit. So far, though, they are refusing to meet unless it's to discuss the possibility of you and Justin having visitation after the adoption."

"Yeah, there's no need to meet under that pretense," Mandi answered in disgust. "We aren't even close to considering that prospect."

"I agree," he said. "I can certainly understand why they are upset though. They kind of got the raw end of this deal as well."

"They did," Mandi conceded, "and I am not trying to take anything away from that. We get that this isn't their fault either, but that doesn't mean we are prepared to give our daughter to them in order to sooth any hard feelings."

"Sure, understood," he assured her, "but I am discovering they really have no idea why the original staffing was overturned. According to Kelly, that information hasn't been shared. So, in their eyes, they're still sort of bewildered by all this. They are assuming the worst about you both based solely on the fact you weren't chosen originally.

"You each present yourselves very well in person," Sam told her, "and I believe getting you all in the same room might break whatever remaining spell this thing has over them."

"Okay, definitely," she agreed, starting to scoop the deviled egg mixture into the egg halves, "just let us know when."

"Well, as I mentioned, we have some work to do to get them to agree, which is the main reason I called you."

"Okay..."

"I would like to share with them the information you gave me about why you weren't selected originally, as well as the objections you presented at the grievance meeting, which ultimately got the decision reversed. I think if we can get them to see you guys were wronged first by the staffing—unfortunately, to the disadvantage of the Nelsons as well—they might start to at least direct their aggravation at the Division rather than at your desire to adopt Jade."

"Sure," Mandi agreed. "We're okay with showing them those

things. I'm honestly surprised it wasn't shared when they were informed the original conclusion had been overturned."

"Are you really?" Sam asked in jest.

Mandi laughed, "Yeah, okay, maybe not."

"Alright, so, very good," Sam wrapped up the call. "I will get Samantha to email those documents to Kelly and let you know what we find out. It would be very good if we can get this thing uncontested by the time it goes to a hearing. It will save time and money."

"We definitely appreciate that," Mandi acknowledged, though she felt compelled to clarify, "What we want most though—no matter the time or the money—is our daughter, so please continue to do whatever you think makes that outcome most likely, regardless of anything else."

"Of course. You and Justin have been extraordinarily good humored and patient so far. I know it's difficult to maintain that composure throughout a process such as this one, but just continue to keep in mind," he reminded her for the tenth time since they had hired him, "that every day Jade is with you is a day in our favor."

9 – Day 302

Susan Richardson looked at the computer screen again, blinking in confusion.

Sitting at her cluttered desk in the state's accounting department, she stared at the conflicting invoices which had arrived with the morning mail. One demanded continued legal financial support for the prospective adoptive parents of a little girl in foster care, Life Number 0911071610. The other stated that all financial support for that family was to be terminated, effective two days prior.

Trying to figure out what was going on, Susan queried the child's life number. Her mouth dropped in astonishment as the results began printing to the screen.

The Division had apparently—at least initially—taken the position they weren't going to support the adoption of the child by her current foster family, but were still sending monthly maintenance checks, which meant the baby was still with that family. The family supported originally moved forward with the adoption, requesting financial assistance, which it was their right to do as the selected family. It seemed CPS then had a change of heart, throwing itself behind the current foster family—who did not request financial assistance—and backing off its promise to help the first. The first family appeared to be

Baby Girl

proceeding despite that, demanding the state fulfill its original obligation.

In the meantime, the legal department for the Division, as well as the Guardian ad Litem's office, had logged over one hundred and fifty hours to the case in the past week alone—work that appeared to be in the interest of both parties, as well as their own obviously shifting interests—contributing to the state paying in excess of $20,000 on the adoption of this one child so far.

That was the kind of money they might pay to get a child away from an abusive or neglectful biological family, yet this little girl's record suggested she had no biological family involved. They had literally had a parent hand them a baby "free and clear," and still managed to rack up tremendous costs despite that.

Susan double-checked the identifying information on each document to make certain she wasn't mistaken.

Case number: *2105-GB12572*
Life number: *0911071610*
Child's name: *Reylco, BG*

It was the same on all of them.

We're spending this kind of money to fight amongst ourselves?

In her five years with the state's accounting office, she had never seen anything like it. With budget cuts and constraints there wasn't a politician or taxpayer alive who wouldn't jump all over this if it came to light during the next audit. In the current climate, in fact, it would be considered nothing short of scandalous.

"Hey Denise," Susan called out, rolling back from the desk, looking over at her supervisor sitting across the aisle.

The woman turned and looked up, her eyebrows raised inquisitively.

"You have to see this."

Denise Saunders sat with the phone pressed to her ear, feeling her aggravation increase with each shrill ring. It wasn't a matter of not caring about whatever the girl's individual circumstance might be, it was that her primary objective was keeping the books balanced. It was their edict for every county in the state.

A line item like twenty thousand dollars in legal fees when a biological parent or family isn't anywhere in sight? When there isn't even an accusation of abuse or neglect or unfit parenting? When the baby was literally dropped off at our doorstep? There is no way to justify the expense. The press will have a field day if they discover this.

And it will be my neck as much as anyone else's.

After the fifth ring, Vanessa Lane, in charge of the Anderson County Child Protective Services Division, answered her phone.

"Hello?"

As soon as she heard the woman's voice, unable to contain her irritation any longer, Denise demanded, "Vanessa, what the *hell* is going on over there?!"

"Ms. Wilson," the older woman began, "I presume you are aware why this meeting has been called?"

"Yes, ma'am," Cheri confirmed calmly from her seat in front of the director's desk. "I believe this is in reference to the Williams-Rice grievance. We overturned the findings of a staffing, designating the existing foster family as the selected adoptive resource for the child in question. There are people who disagree with our decision."

"That's correct," she responded, shuffling through some papers. "As you are also likely aware, it was Leslie Franklin who appealed the verdict of you and your supervisor on this matter. Valerie Francis, correct?"

"Yes," Cheri confirmed, "my supervisor is Valerie and I am aware it is Leslie who appealed."

"Does Leslie report to you?"

"She does," Cheri nodded.

"Did she share with you the reasons for the appeal?"

"She did."

"What were the reasons she gave?"

Taking a deep breath, Cheri replied, "Her opinion is that if the original staffing was found to be in error, then another staffing — with all new prospective families — should have been scheduled rather than us not only tossing out the decision but also selecting the Williams-Rice family. There seems to be some concern that Valerie Francis and I, with approval from Vanessa Lane, decided on the foster family without consulting anyone else."

"Do you feel her reasons are valid?"

"I have respect for Leslie," Cheri conveyed to the woman. "I know it takes a great deal of integrity to stand up for what we believe, especially when it's not what those we report to might condone. Having said that, though, I don't think she has a full understanding of the situation and, therefore, I don't agree with the appeal."

"So, to be clear, at this point you stand behind the resolution reached as a result of the grievance?"

"I do."

"Alright, let's get started then. Will you summarize for me why you and Valerie came to the decision you did after meeting with Ms.

Williams and Mr. Rice?"

Nodding, Cheri started, "First and foremost, the primary justification for denying Justin Rice and Mandi Williams as Baby Girl's adoptive resource was proven to be unsubstantiated."

"And what was that reason?"

"The claim there had been a hotline against them related to spanking a child in their care almost a year before."

"There wasn't?"

"There was no hotline," Cheri shook her head, pursing her lips. "I searched our records—electronic and otherwise—, I interviewed the people involved, and there was nothing."

Puzzled, the woman asked, "Where did the claim come from then?"

"That remains a mystery," Cheri admitted, "but I am looking into it. Near as I have been able to figure out, it seems to have originated with the Guardian ad Litem, though she—Edith Scarlett—can't seem to recall exactly where she heard it from."

The woman nodded, taking notes. "Was there anything else?"

"As far as the official reasons given, that was the only one of significance. The other two reasons were relatively minor. The first seemed to be that the Guardian ad Litem, Edith, felt the foster mother didn't answer in depth enough about her own mother's death when she was a teenager. The second issue seemed to revolve around whether the Williams-Rice family requested the removal of a foster child from their home for selfish reason. It was the same foster child the hotline was supposedly in relation to."

"Removal of the child was requested because...?"

"Apparently he could not be trusted around the family dog without attempting to harm it. I checked with his therapist at the time and these incidents with the animal are well documented. They went on for almost the entire duration of his stay with the family. After several months, when everyone had run out of ideas, they felt they had no choice but to ask that he be placed in a more suitable home."

The woman grimaced, "That's a shame."

Cheri nodded, "It is, but there's no evidence they were flippant or callous about their decision. The primary reason we overturned the staffing is because the information the attendees had was either completely inaccurate or twisted in some way. The reality is there is no significant justification for moving the child."

"Why weren't they able to reach the same determination during the staffing?"

"I believe it was a combination of things," Cheri theorized.

"Such as?"

"Their licensing manager was absent due to being on leave for surgery. The woman standing in for her didn't know the foster family very well and was ill-equipped, in my opinion, to assist in clearing up any misinformation. I also got the impression the environment at the staffing wasn't conducive to having a productive conversation."

"Ms. Wilson," the woman sighed, removing her glasses to rub the bridge of her nose, "you have been with the Division for the past twenty years and I have a great deal of respect for what you have brought to this agency as well as for your opinion on matters such as these. You have been out in the field, in the office, all over this organization. You have always conducted yourself in a manner that is both professional and very noticeably intent upon protecting the best interests of the children in our custody."

"Thank you."

"I also did some research into this case and, like you, found nothing that seems to warrant removing the child from her current placement. I see no reason her existing family can't continue to provide a protective, loving environment for her. If, in addition, you met with them and continue to hold that belief, then I am satisfied with your decision and will uphold the grievance findings."

Cheri nodded, saying again, "Thank you."

"Having said that," the woman continued, "I'm sure it isn't lost on you how awful this might appear to some."

"I do realize there has been backlash related to this," Cheri acknowledged, "but the grievance process was put in place to handle the fact that while we are an agency of mostly good-intentioned people, we are people none-the-less. Specifically, we are imperfect people, bound to make mistakes for one reason or another. I've heard some claim that our overturning the decision is proof the system has failed, but the system includes this process, the ability to appeal. It's the net and I am of the opinion it worked as intended in this instance. There might have been an oversight, a hiccup, but I don't believe it has failed."

"I understand your point," the woman conceded, "and, certainly, I don't ever want us to not correct a wrong simply because accountability isn't always convenient or comfortable. That's not in anyone's best long term interest either."

"Definitely not."

"However, what I would like us to figure out is how to make this sort of error during a staffing less likely," she pushed. "Too many things went awry here to not believe that at least some of them could have been preventable."

"I know what you mean," Cheri said. "We are starting to look into entirely changing the way staffings work—"

"Correct me if I'm wrong, but I believe the transformations you are referring to have been at the discussion phase for the better part of a year," the woman remarked dryly, "yet they have not materialized."

Knowing there was nothing she could say to refute the observation, Cheri decided it was wisest to say nothing.

Sighing, the woman asked, "Do you believe the new process might have helped prevent this scenario?"

"Honestly," Cheri told her, "I don't know that it would have. The issue in this case seems to have more to do with the tone of the staffing—which is set by the participants, not the applicants—which, more and more, we are hearing is intimidating in nature. Also…" she hesitated.

"What is it, Ms. Wilson?"

"This family heard from another party that the result of the staffing was actually decided before the meeting ever commenced."

"Is that true?"

Shrugging, Cheri answered truthfully, "I suspect it might be, but I don't have proof of that. I do know the staffings lately have been getting done in record time. In a lot of these cases maybe it's not terrible if everyone talks before and figures things out, but it was certainly not helpful in this situation. Here the conclusions seem to have been drawn before the validity of the information had even been determined, including prior to anyone having an opportunity to adequately interview the existing foster family."

"I would certainly hope we are being extra cautious in any instance where we are contemplating removing a child from their existing caregiver, especially if it's one we appointed to begin with," the woman replied grimly.

"I agree and that is my expectation as well," Cheri assured her.

Juli L. Idleman

"We cannot be too thorough in situations such as these. It shouldn't be too much to give our own families the same courtesy we extend the biological families of these kids, especially when they haven't been accused of anything nearly as serious."

10 – Day 326

"I have to tell you," Sam started as soon as Mandi answered her phone, "this is one of the strangest cases I think I've ever been part of. I mean, there have been some strange ones, but this really has to be in the top handful."

Mandi laughed nervously, "What happened now?"

She had barely arrived at work for the day when her phone notified her of Sam's incoming call.

"Well, you know I, the DFS attorney, the Guardian ad Litem and the Nelsons' attorney are all supposed to spend today conducting witness interviews in preparation for the upcoming hearing."

"Right…" Mandi felt her tummy twist nervously.

"So there was a lot of confusion trying to confirm whether or not these meetings were even going to happen. I decided to show up anyway, as did the CPS attorneys and Payton Gringo from the Guardian ad Litems' office, but the Nelsons' attorney, Kelly, isn't here."

"Okay…"

"In her absence, I have been able to spend some time chatting with the CPS attorney, Jamie Lockheed, and her supervisor, Katrina Logan. I just finished a very interesting discussion with them in fact."

"Okay," Mandi said again, hesitantly.

"I guess they have been under quite a bit of pressure from the state capital to get this thing resolved."

Eyes widening in surprise, Mandi responded, "Really?"

"Yeah, which... I mean, I'm sure it has the potential to be an embarrassing nightmare for them."

"I have no doubt," Mandi agreed.

"When I last spoke with Kelly yesterday afternoon, I kind of got the feeling something was up. She seemed to have lost some of her original steam. I pressed her on it a bit and, come to find out, the Nelsons finally had an opportunity to review all of the documentation we provided them on the original staffing and why it was overturned, as well as your home study. It sounded as if they were starting to realize that the staffing process really failed in this instance; that you and Justin didn't pursue having it overturned out of simple bitterness or resentment, but because it was truly erroneous."

"Right," Mandi confirmed.

Not that there isn't a degree of bitterness and resentment, though it's never really been at the Nelsons.

"We left it that we would proceed with the witness interviews this morning, since they have been scheduled for several weeks and it's hard to get time with a number of these individuals, but it seemed as if no one on their side really had their heart in it anymore."

"Well, that's good," Mandi said, feeling cautiously hopeful.

"As agreed, though, I showed up for the witness interviews this morning only to find Kelly not here. That's when Jamie and Katrina filled me in on the rest. Apparently, she's waiting for word on whether or not the Division is going to agree to some things her clients have asked for in exchange for dropping their case. My understanding is that the delay on getting an answer is CPS waiting for word from the capital on whether or not they can comply."

Since her eyebrows couldn't shoot any further off her head, Mandi's jaw dropped. Dumbfounded, she asked, "What are they wanting?"

"I'm not entirely certain," Sam answered. "They didn't share that with me, but I would imagine it's compensation for legal fees, possibly punitive damages."

Mandi wondered if the Nelsons' requests would be granted. Even if they weren't, it occurred to her that the Nelsons had already considerably weakened their position simply by asking.

Doesn't this prove our point that, regardless of whether or not the Nelsons are good people, they have no emotional attachment to Jade or her to them? There is nothing any bureaucratic body could offer that would cause us to consider dropping our fight for her.

Where Mandi and Justin had shelled out tens of thousands of dollars on a fifty-percent chance they might be able to keep their daughter, the Nelsons were willing to barter her for their financial gain. They were probably justified in their indignation, but—most importantly to Mandi—it seemed to confirm they had zero sincere interest in the specific little girl who had stolen the hearts of them, their family and friends.

"So I guess that's what we are waiting on now," Sam interrupted her thoughts. "Word from the Division and the state capital. We have postponed the witness interviews until this afternoon with the hope they won't even be necessary. There is supposed to be a conference call in an hour to find out if the Nelsons are going to be granted their requests. I don't expect it to be a quick call, but I will get in touch as soon as we are done."

Still trying to process everything, Mandi answered hastily, "Okay, sounds good. Thanks, Sam."

"Truly one of the most bizarre cases I have ever been involved with…" he repeated once again before hanging up.

"So they are essentially open to a bribe now?" Kelsey asked at lunch.

"Yeah, that's the same thing Justin and I are thinking. Even if they don't back off at this point — we should know by the end of the day — it shows their motivation is mostly anger at CPS. Anger which might be justified, but that has nothing to do with a genuine desire to try and figure out what's in Jade's best interests."

Kelsey shook her head, "This is insanity."

"Yeah, no kidding," Mandi responded with a short laugh. After a second, she added, "For the record, as a taxpayer, I'm relieved there are people in our capital at least paying enough attention to our tax dollars that they must have realized what a spectacular waste this is. Justin and I still have to absorb most of the cost associated with our attorney — already at a staggering amount in less than two months — but the state is also having to absorb its own rising costs as well… just to fight a family they paid to investigate and certify to begin with."

Kelsey nodded, swallowing a bite of sandwich and asking, "So is it essentially just a battle between you and the Nelsons? Or, if they suddenly back out, are you still not assured of being Jade's adoptive parents?"

"They are our biggest hurdle at this point, mostly because their presence is forcing everyone to exert a lot of extra time and energy. Nothing will be final until the commissioner says it is… but the Nelsons backing off would certainly put this on a much more normal,

Baby Girl

much less stressful path. It would make success almost a certainty."

"That's what we'll hope for then," Kelsey commented.

Mandi smiled, "Definitely."

"My clients are going to be very pleased by this news," Sam conveyed to both Jamie and Katrina as he shook their hands. "Thank you both so much for your hard work over the last several days in particular."

"We're just glad to finally start putting it behind us," Katrina said. "I assume you'll be scheduling an adoption hearing in the next month or so? How old is Baby Girl now?"

"Almost eleven months," he answered, after giving it some thought. "Yes, our intention is to get this in front of the commissioner as soon as possible. In fact, I need to excuse myself to see if I can catch Payton before she leaves. I've left a couple messages for her and haven't heard back. I'm hoping, now that the Nelsons have dismissed their case, she will agree to have this put on the uncontested docket."

"Sure," Katrina responded. "We'll let you get going. Please be sure to let us know if you need anything else."

"Most certainly," he agreed, turning away. "Thank you again."

With a slight jog, he headed in the direction he'd last seen Payton walking. He found her talking to a colleague. As he approached, they finished their conversation and moved as if to leave.

"Payton," he called out. "Hey Payton, do you have a minute?"

Reluctantly, the woman bade her co-worker good-bye and stopped to wait for Sam.

"I was hoping you might have a few minutes to discuss the Reylco case. As you are aware, I am representing the Williams-Rice family." Trying to gauge her position, he asked with a sincere smile, "This has been quite a wild ride so far, hasn't it?"

"It has," she agreed, without betraying any emotion.

"Our next step would normally be to request an adoption hearing," Sam continued carefully, "unless there are issues or questions your office would like us to attend to first."

Payton wasn't quite certain how to answer Sam's inquiry. She'd been hoping to avoid him until she had a chance to see what thoughts Edith had on this latest development.

Surely she will be ready to back off.

"I might call one or two people from the staffing," Payton said uncertainly.

"Is there some lingering concern about my clients," he wondered, offering, "and, if so, anything we can do to assist in clearing it up?"

"I would just like to make certain we've represented or covered any issues raised at the original staffing," she stonewalled.

"Are you aware of what those issues were?"

Feeling tense, Payton said shortly, "I will review their file extensively before the adoption hearing, of course."

"Alright," Sam responded with a thoughtful nod. He knew that aggravating Payton wasn't in their best interests. "I just wanted to offer you our assistance in getting your hands on any documents or information pertaining to my clients. We obviously fully believe that the original staffing was in error. The fact it was overturned and the events of today seem to be further proof of that fact."

"I understand your position," Payton assured Sam with a tight smile.

"Also, have you had an opportunity to meet with Mandi, Justin or Jade?"

"No, I haven't," the woman admitted.

Sam smiled patiently, "I know my clients would jump out windows in order to afford you every opportunity to get to know them and Jade in order to assist in facilitating your decision. If you'd like me to set up a meeting at the office or a home visit, please just let me know. Mandi and Justin are attempting to be as transparent as possible so that everyone gets the chance to, hopefully, put any concerns to rest before the hearing."

Payton found Sam tiring, or maybe it was just the case. She responded, "Sure, I will let you know if I feel there's a need to do that."

"Do you want me to wait before requesting this be added to Commissioner Robert's docket?"

Shaking her head, she answered, "No, there's no reason to hold that up."

"Should we put it on the contested or uncontested docket?"

Payton thought about it, then replied slowly, "I think we can probably put it on the uncontested docket. My witnesses shouldn't take more than ten minutes, so unless you plan to call an extensive number of witnesses…"

"No, maybe just one or two to refute yours, if necessary."

Payton nodded.

"Do you know which witnesses you plan to call?"

"Not yet," she answered. "I need to give it some thought, talk to a few individuals to see who might be best."

"Do you mind sending me your witness list once you have it finalized?" Sam requested.

"That's no problem. I will email it to you by the end of this week."

"Thanks," he replied. "I'll be on the lookout for it and will follow-up if I have any questions."

Sam had a bad feeling walking away from the conversation with Payton, but as he reached for his phone he decided not to mention it to the Williams-Rice family. He didn't want his skepticism to overshadow what was otherwise fabulous news.

"Hello?"

"Mandi," Sam greeted his client jovially, "do you have a bottle of champagne handy?"

"I can't believe they backed out," Edith hissed, shaking her head as she slid in across the table from Payton.

"It was a lot for them to put up with," she replied, knowing Edith was referring to the text she had sent regarding the Reylco case. "The Nelsons have never even met the child."

"We can't let this be the end of it," Edith said with conviction, picking up her menu. "The Williams-Rice family still doesn't deserve that little girl. I'll be damned if I'm going to let this clear the road for them."

Payton looked down at the table briefly, before looking back up and stating, "Their attorney wants to get the adoption hearing scheduled. I already told him he could request it for the uncontested docket."

Edith's jaw dropped in disbelief. After a moment, she recovered herself, demanding incredulously, "What do you mean you told him they could put it on the uncontested docket? Why would you say a thing like that?"

"I'm sorry, he cornered me and I didn't have time to catch up with you. I honestly didn't think you would want to persist with this once you found out the Nelsons withdrew," Payton answered uncomfortably. "This *is* the only family who knows her, Edith."

Baby Girl

"She's too young to know any different," Edith retorted, brushing the observation aside. "You're not going to support their petition."

"On what grounds?" Payton implored, wishing the woman would just drop the issue.

"Find something," Edith shrugged. "Ask evocative questions. Put them on the defensive. Place a seed of doubt in the commissioner's mind about their suitability as parents, one just significant enough he can't quite ignore but not so significant anyone can really prove or disprove anything. It doesn't matter what you do," she said in frustration, "as long as they don't get that baby."

After a slight pause, Edith's eyes lit up suddenly, "I've got it!"

"What?"

"Read back through their home study. There was something there..." she tried to remember, "The mother. Her mother died as a teenager and a few years ago she went to talk to a psychologist."

"Is she still seeing one?"

Edith shook her head, "I think she said she only went once or twice—"

"There's no way—"

"—but I know there's something there you can use. All you have to do is suggest the potential of mental instability, Payton, and it will be enough to send everything and everyone into a tailspin. No commissioner will want to risk the implications of what you'll be hypothesizing."

"I don't know, Edith," Payton replied skeptically.

Exasperated, the other woman demanded, "What exactly don't you know?"

"There is no evidence anything like that is really an issue—"

"Just do it," Edith replied in annoyance. "Make them doubt even themselves. They think they can challenge me? They had no right to do what they did. They should have accepted the outcome of the staffing, trusting that we know what's best for these kids.

"Maybe the Division is willing to back down and maybe that raggedy couple we chose—I guess I was wrong about them after all—is willing to back down, but I'm not about to. They have no right to that child," she hissed vehemently. "We are completely within the law looking out for the best interests of that little girl. You let their attorney know the case will be going on the contested docket. Period."

Payton called the family court clerk rather than the Williams-Rice attorney. She didn't want to field all the questions she knew Sam would have about her apparent change of heart.

"Hi, Nancy," she greeted the woman who had been with the courts for more than a couple decades. "I wanted to put a bug in your ear about a case that's coming your way, supposed to be scheduling an adoption hearing."

"Okay," Nancy answered, "What's the case number?"

"2-1-0-5-G-B-1-2-5-7-2."

"Alright," the clerk prompted after the case file loaded on the screen in front of her, "What's the note?"

"Make certain the adoption hearing gets scheduled on the contested docket," she told the woman. "It is not uncontested. I have a feeling the attorney might try to slide it onto the wrong docket."

"Sure thing, Payton," Nancy agreed. "I know how those lawyers can be. I've got it noted."

11 – Day 357

"We have run into a bit of a snag," Sam said with resignation, a preemptively placating smile on his lips.

Mandi felt her stomach turn. They had hoped today would be the day their adoption of Jade would be final, but that wish had been squashed when Payton unexpectedly threw a temper tantrum at the start of the adoption hearing. She claimed to have not had time to review the home study to determine whether or not Justin and Mandi were suitable parents.

Sam — appearing more aggravated than they had ever seen him — pointed out that the home study had been on file and therefore available to her for the three weeks preceding. He also testily pointed out that they had offered numerous times to let Payton visit the Williams-Rice home in order to assist in her efforts to evaluate the placement. The confrontation was hostile enough for Commissioner Roberts to request the courtroom be cleared while he conferred with counsel.

Twenty minutes later, the attorneys had finally emerged, Sam looking grim. Justin and Mandi had shot disappointed glances at each other as he made his way over.

"What's the snag?" Mandi asked, trying not to sound as

pessimistic as she felt.

"It's completely ludicrous, but..." Sam hesitated, "the Guardian ad Litem brought up your mother passing away."

Puzzled, Mandi looked at Justin. She could see he was also perplexed. Looking back at Kendal, she said, "Okay."

"Well, first, if you'll bear with me," Sam said, appearing to have had another thought, "let me backtrack a bit to a conversation I had with Cheri Wilson right before the hearing. Do you remember her?"

"Of course. She was one of the individuals in our grievance meeting," Justin said as Mandi nodded.

"Right," he confirmed. "Well, she and I aren't used to finding ourselves on the same side at these things—as I discussed with you during our first meeting most of my cases start out against the Division and never experience the sides changing as it did here. So we were afforded a rare opportunity to compare notes today. Come to find out, Cheri and Valerie had to go to the state capital to defend overturning the staffing."

"Wow," Mandi commented, surprised. She had never realized there was any risk the grievance verdict might be overturned. In hindsight, she was grateful they hadn't known and had therefore been spared the stress of worrying about it.

"Exactly," he agreed. "Obviously their decision was upheld, but Cheri shed additional light on what might be at work behind the scenes of all this. From what she indicated, it sounds as if your specific case has gotten caught up in a political battle going on between the Division and the Guardian ad Litem's office. Specifically, there has been tension between the two groups related to procedure. I guess all the missteps surrounding your case kind of brought that conflict to a boiling point and it's now become something of a case-in-point for the

Guardian ad Litem's office."

"In fact, things have been so tense between the two groups that a workgroup was even set up with the explicit purpose of bettering relations between the two agencies. I guess the woman with CPS who appealed the grievance result—Leslie—is a part of that group and particularly sympathetic to the Guardian ad Litem's office. Cheri believes she was pressured into appealing your selection. Again, more because the GAL is angry about process than that they have any legitimate objection to you individually."

"Huh," Justin commented. "So what does that mean for the adoption? I gather it's not going to happen today, but... what next? We can't be expected to solve hard feelings between two already disparate groups of people, can we?"

"Well, unfortunately," Sam said with a sigh, "it doesn't change anything we have to do, except perhaps confirm our lingering suspicions that there was more going on here than we were aware of. It was, after all, unbelievable that any of these agencies would ever have opposed you so vigorously while at the same time making no effort to visit or force the court to move her. To me that says they must know Jade is in a perfectly safe environment."

"So we're stuck between two groups who are at odds with each other on issues that have nothing to do with Jade," Mandi grimaced, "and while they battle, we continue to pay on every front."

"Pretty much," Sam conceded. "I wanted to share that with you because it might give more context to what just happened in the courtroom. You are both good people, and I don't want you to take any of this too personally." He was speaking to them both, but looking at Mandi.

Shifting uncomfortably, she answered, "Okay."

"As I started to say a minute ago," he went on, "the Guardian ad Litem—who is particularly upset about the outcome of the grievance—brought up your mother passing away. I guess you mentioned in your home study that you were put on anti-anxiety medicine initially."

"That's correct," Mandi confirmed. "They took me off of them after a couple of months because I was dealing with everything pretty well, you know, considering."

"Right," he nodded.

Mandi wasn't entirely certain where the conversation was going, but it made her uneasy nonetheless. "Is that a problem? I mean, I was fifteen. It was more than half a lifetime ago. Surely…"

"Also in the home study," he continued hesitantly, "you mentioned visiting a psychiatrist six years ago."

Until it had been brought up at the staffing, Mandi had almost forgotten about the visit.

"That's right," she responded slowly. "I lost a good friend of mine in an automobile accident. It was so eerily similar to my mother's death… It seemed like the proactive thing to do in order to make certain I had resources in place in the event it stirred up any old feelings."

"Did the individual prescribe you anti-anxiety medication?"

Mandi answered truthfully, "The short answer is yes. The long answer is that I was only looking for someone to talk to, someone without personal or professional connections to my life. The office my insurance company sent me to had a psychiatrist, but I never spoke to him. Instead, I spoke with the nurse practitioner.

"I told her medication wasn't really what I was looking for. She went ahead and prescribed an anti-anxiety medicine, telling me that I could take it if I needed and to come back and see her in a month. I

Baby Girl

didn't fill the prescription, but I did take it with me. I didn't want to burn that bridge because I truly didn't know what I might need at that point."

"Understandable," Sam said.

"In the next month, I started working out more, finding healthy outlets for my grief. I went back for the thirty day appointment anyway — it was really just a quick 'how are you doing' fifteen minute discussion. I told her I was doing fine. I don't remember discussing the script or claiming to take the medicine, but I can't say she didn't assume I was either. I remember she wrote me another one for a 90-day supply just in case. I didn't fill that one either. I guess I just thought I would keep the option. I didn't end up using it and I never went back after the second visit."

"I figured it was probably something like that," Sam nodded with satisfaction, "and it sounds as if you handled things well, same as you did with your mother, simply trying to make certain nothing from the past derailed you."

Mandi nodded. His understanding wasn't doing much to abate her sense of apprehension.

"What's the problem here?" Justin finally cut in flatly, "I don't mean to be rude, and I hope you realize it's not directed at you personally, but we're talking about incidents that occurred quite awhile ago. What have they got to do with the fact we all just got kicked out of the courtroom and it doesn't appear the adoption is going to be finalized today?"

Sam sighed. He couldn't put it off any longer.

"The Guardian ad Litem, Payton, has suggested to the commissioner that you have taken yourself off medication against doctor's orders."

Mandi's jaw dropped. She didn't know how to respond.

"What?!" Justin exclaimed, suffering no such loss of speech, his eyes wide in shock, "That's ridiculous!"

Sam agreed, "It's legal posturing. As Cheri shared with me earlier and as I just shared with you, there is more going on here than what we see. We all know this has nothing to do with Jade. As I said, if they were really concerned she wouldn't be with you, they would have objected to our motion to keep her there, and they sure wouldn't be putting off visits to check on her. On the contrary, they would be all over you. Yet they aren't."

He shook his head, repeating, "No, there's more to this, just as Cheri indicated. I'm going to make some calls to try to find out if there's anything else going on."

Both Mandi and Justin nodded.

"In the meantime, unfortunately," Sam looked at Mandi, "you're going to have to get a psychological evaluation to refute what Payton has put out there."

Mandi grimaced, "Nice."

"I know." Sam reassured her, "I have no doubt you'll knock the evaluation out of the park. You are some of my most put together clients — especially given the strain of this particular case — and you have never failed to find the positive. I am confident the evaluation will ultimately only be a benefit to us."

Blushing, Mandi didn't know what to say. She felt as if maybe he had been misled. While it was true both she and Justin tended to find the upside to most situations that didn't mean they — at least certainly *she* — didn't do their share of screaming and stomping and crying first.

"We'll probably have you included in the evaluation as well," Sam warned Justin, "in the event they turn their attack dogs on you next."

"Sure," Justin agreed.

"Any skeletons in your closet I should be aware of?" Sam teased, trying to lighten the mood.

Giving a disgusted laugh, filled with disappointment, Justin shook his head, "I don't think so."

"I believe this is just an inconvenience," Sam told them, their sober faces making him serious once again, "not something that will ultimately put the adoption in jeopardy. We merely have to play their game until we figure out exactly what game it is they're playing. Unfortunately, it's going to add time and, of course, you will need to pay for the evaluation. Is that going to be a problem?"

"No," Mandi said as Justin shook his head.

"Good," Sam responded. "I will get it set up and have Samantha call you with the details. In the meantime, you guys hang in there. Remember that every day she is with you is a day in your favor."

"Sure," Mandi appreciated the reminder, recognized the truth of his words, though hearing it was starting to feel a little hollow.

The days are getting long, tedious and expensive.

It was becoming very clear the state had no reason to handle the matter of Jade's life with any sense of sincere inquiry or urgency.

"I can't imagine what it must be like," Justin said as they were about to go their separate ways in the court parking lot. Both were on their way back to their respective offices.

"What's that?" Mandi wondered distractedly, pulled from the thoughts she had been lost in.

"To have people not let you move beyond your past," he answered.

"Oh," Mandi nodded, grimly, "yeah."

"I mean," he continued wistfully, with a slight shake of his head, "they are totally missing the point. It shouldn't be about who you *were*, but about who you *are*. Instead of trying to summon or shape you into the fifteen-year-old, which is exactly what it feels like they're trying to do," he waved his hand in her general direction, "they ought to be in awe of the thirty-year-old."

Mandi felt tears burn her eyes unexpectedly. She gave Justin a hug, "Thank you."

"I'm serious," Justin laughed in embarrassment, returning the hug. "I'm actually really concerned I'll do worse on any psychological evaluation than you will."

Laughing, Mandi said as she stepped away, "Let's hope they get it out of their system with me."

Justin took the opportunity to ask seriously, "Are you having any second thoughts about the fact we decided to fight for Jade?"

"None," Mandi answered immediately. "It hurts that it's so difficult, it's frustrating that it makes so little sense, I very much want it to be done with and concluded in our favor... but I don't regret it at all. You?"

"Not at all," he replied.

Later that afternoon, Sam called Mandi to let her know Samantha had scheduled a time in three weeks—the earliest available appointment—for them to meet with the forensic psychologist.

"I went ahead and called you rather than having Samantha," he explained, "because I want to let you know how we've set things up."

"Sure."

"Although I don't believe we're going to have any problems, the protocol with these types of evaluations is for our firm to retain the psychologist. This means we pay him and he will report his findings directly to us, rather than to you."

Mandi's brow furrowed in confusion. As if reading her mind, Sam went on to clarify, "I will, of course, share the findings with you and Justin. The reason we do it this way is that even though we don't have to submit the evaluation to court—let's say in the unlikely event the assessment is unfavorable—, the opposing counsel can still subpoena you to testify about the findings. However, if I receive the results and determine they aren't in our best interests, I can opt not to share the details with you and, as your attorney, also can't be called to testify against you."

"I see," Mandi said, with a nod.

"So, it's really for your own protection, even though I truly don't believe it will be necessary. Does that make sense?"

"It does."

"Now, the retainer the doctor has requested for this case is eight thousand dollars. I know you have been paying your bill in full each month. Can you include an additional eight with the next one?"

Mandi's mind stumbled over the amount, but her response was automatic, "Sure, we can do that. We'll put it in the mail today."

"Great, that's just great," he said encouragingly. "As soon as we get it, we'll cut a check to his office. It should get to him well before your appointment."

After hanging up with Sam, Mandi walked over to her desk. She sighed and shook her head, looking absently at the wall.

She had known this moment was coming. As much cost as they had cut from their everyday lives, Sam was working on Jade's case almost non-stop. It had been taking every bit of their monthly disposable income to keep up with the invoices from Kendal &

Kendal. So far, they had paid a little over twenty-two thousand dollars, including their initial retainer. They had known they wouldn't be able to absorb much more.

Mandi realized that borrowing from their retirement accounts wasn't the end of the world, but it added to the insult of the entire situation in a way nothing else had.

Sure, we should be grateful to have the resources to take this on, she told herself, *but it doesn't change the aggravation over the fact it's money we shouldn't have to spend.*

Mandi reflected on the conversation with Sam, specifically the information Cheri had shared with him.

To think this is some political battle, that the future of our family hinges on things that have nothing to do with our worth or our ability is more disturbing than the original fear that perhaps they recognized in us a glaring defect we were incapable of seeing. At least the latter was something we might have had a hope of addressing.

This? Political posturing at the expense of our family rather than a sincere desire to determine Jade's best interests? Offering us no recourse except to keep writing the checks, playing the game, and waiting? It is frustrating, even infuriating.

Mandi sighed.

The waiting is getting unbearable.

Having seen Edith from across the lunchroom, the spry sixty-seven-year-old licensing manager walked briskly over to the table. She had returned from medical leave the day before, gotten up-to-speed on all her cases and left with one specific goal for today: a personal conversation with Edith Scarlett.

Seeing her approach, Edith greeted, "Hi Jean, how—"

"What are you doing with the Williams-Rice case?" Jean asked angrily, interrupting the pleasantries.

Taken aback, Edith answered, "I'm sure I don't know—"

"You do know," Jean hissed, sliding into the chair next to her at the round table, leaning in.

"Jean, the dramatics are a bit much, don't you think?" Edith remarked, feigning embarrassment for the woman.

Ignoring the comment, Jean demanded, "Do you honestly feel that baby is at risk of any harm from them?"

"Nobody has said that," Edith replied in a soothing, yet condescending tone. "It's just that we can never be too careful when it comes to the placement of one of these children, don't you agree?"

"Yes, we can," Jean shot back at the younger woman, knowing it wasn't the answer she was expecting, refusing to fall for her games. "We can absolutely be too careful to the point we alienate and harm the wrong people. Do you not feel I did my job adequately when I researched and licensed the family?"

With an exasperated sigh, Edith responded, "Oh, Jean, is that what this is about? Please don't take our unwillingness to support them as a personal critique of your efforts. You don't have to—"

"Look here," Jean cut her off, pointing her crooked finger in the direction of the arrogant Guardian ad Litem, "your mind games might work on others, but you and I are a couple of the oldest birds in this joint. So cut the crap. We both know this has nothing to do with my work, a sincere fear for that girl's safety or even with the Williams-Rice family."

"Is that so?"

"Yes, that is so," she retorted. "This has to do with you trying to mold the law to support your own rigid, biased, personal beliefs about what constitutes a family. It's not the first time I've seen you do it and it's a wonder you get away with it, but this is the first time you've made the mistake of messing with one of my families."

"Talk to my supervisor if you have complaints," Edith said dismissively. She was uncomfortable by the bluntness of the licensing manager, but also apathetic. "If you don't mind, I'd like to get back to my lunch now."

"I'm not going to go to your supervisor," Jean told her in disgust. "We both know it would be a waste of time, as you have too many friends in powerful positions."

Edith smirked, "My, but you do have an imagination, don't you? Too many daytime soaps during your leave?"

"There are already questions about you, Edith," Jean went on, ignoring her remark, "You don't control every one up the chain. People outside your sphere of influence are starting to notice things. That hotline story? The folks at the state capital want to know where that fabricated line of bull came from. All roads lead back to you. The common theme to some of our most contentious and heartbreaking cases? You." Jean laughed derisively, repeating, "People are starting to notice. It's only a matter of time. Are you really so foolish as to believe you are untouchable?

"I can tell you this," Jean continued without giving her an opportunity to respond, "you had better watch it because if you keep messing with this family, if they *lose* this baby and I can prove you made any of it up, I won't go to your supervisor but directly to the Board to have your license to practice law revoked."

"You wouldn't—"

"Are you certain?" Jean snapped, "I'm an old, old lady, Edith. I could have retired years ago. You can't threaten my career the way you can these college kids running around here trying to keep their noses clean so they can get a little work experience on their resume. Seeing you stripped of the right to abuse the laws meant to give these kids a second chance might be just the incentive I need to make certain I leave here on a high note. Or at least a very memorable one."

Having said her piece, Jean got up and walked away from the table satisfied. Edith pursed her lips unhappily as she watched the woman's retreating figure.

12 – Day 381

When Mandi arrived at daycare to pick up the kids, she realized Jade's biological father was there holding her. She couldn't get to her baby, who was nestled in the man's arms, but instead leaned in through a small window in the wall separating her from the rest of the center.

Seeing Mandi, the office manager came over to greet her. Rather than being put out by the presence of the individual holding Jade, the woman was smiling as if nothing out of the ordinary was happening.

"Has he been here all day?" Mandi hissed, once the other woman stepped up to the barrier that was keeping her out.

"Oh, yeah," Anna's smiled widened, "He's really great."

Mandi's eyebrows shot up in surprise.

"He's been by every day this week in fact," Anna told her, glancing over at the man fondly.

"He has?"

What is going on?

"Yeah," she continued, "and Jade's caseworker was here earlier today. She just loves him."

"She was? Who does? The caseworker?" Mandi's mind was spinning.

Dawn usually always notifies us when she plans a visit to either our home or daycare.

Nodding enthusiastically, Anna said, "I think they are going to start looking into setting up visitation for the two of them. I guess he's really gotten his act together this past year."

"Why didn't anyone tell us he was coming by?"

"Well, he has a right, doesn't he?"

"No, he doesn't," Mandi shot back automatically, indignantly.

Does he?

Anna just stared at her blankly, clearly puzzled as to what Mandi found so distressing. The barrier between them felt as if it could be measured in miles rather than inches.

"He's her father," Anna pointed out in confusion.

Glancing past the woman, Mandi looked at the baby curled up in the man's arms.

If he has returned and has really gotten his life together, shouldn't I be happy for Jade?

Another thought countered, *But she's been with us her whole life. We love her so much.*

Mandi's anger dissolved into the most intense, conflicted sadness she had ever felt. It made her throat ache, squeezed the air from her lungs, causing her entire body to tense from the strain of trying to withstand it.

Anna continued to remain oblivious to what was so difficult about the situation.

It's uncharacteristic of her to be so calloused.

"It's just going to be so hard to give her up," Mandi tried to explain. It was all she could choke out before the pain made it impossible to continue. She turned away from the window, her vision blurring, unable to hold back any longer the huge sob that shook her body.

We have lost her. After everything we've been through, we lost her anyway. He hasn't been here fighting for her like we have, yet now he gets to show up and just take her. She's our child. Will no one acknowledge she's our child?

The room started to spin.

Why is Jade a baby?

As if being yanked backward through the air, Mandi abruptly found herself sprawled across the bed on her stomach.

It didn't happen.

Relief washed over her.

After a moment, she pushed herself up to head for the shower. It seemed her mind was getting better about freeing itself from these horrible dreams, but she longed for the day when they would stop entirely.

"It should be illegal, what they are doing to you guys," Kelsey grimaced, shaking her head. "What time is the evaluation?"

She was sitting at the chair in her office, taking a break from an especially busy day. In between meetings, she had decided to call Mandi to find out the latest on the adoption.

"Two," Mandi responded, answering the last question before the first statement, to which she admitted, "It's difficult having to go back and pull up all this stuff that happened so long ago. It's hard to explain, but it's like being forced to suffer through it all over again."

"I bet."

Having taken the day off work for the psychological evaluation later in the afternoon, Kelsey's call had caught Mandi in the midst of putting laundry away. She had plopped down on the bed in the master bedroom as she turned her attention to answering her friend's questions.

Attempting to explain herself further, Mandi went on, "Don't get me wrong. I certainly think about my mother, but I stopped dwelling on the details of it a long time ago. The same with Cindy's car accident. To answer some of these questions now, to remember the details they are asking about, I really have to put myself back there... and that's actually kind of traumatic, more so than even I would have expected."

"Nobody would want to relive something like that," Kelsey comforted, her voice grim, "especially when the people asking aren't looking to be supportive but to derive some weakness."

"I think that's exactly what makes it so difficult," Mandi agreed. "This isn't the kind of stuff a person opens up to just anyone about, least of all individuals whose stated objective is to take away one of the people I love most in the world."

"Exactly."

Mandi grimaced, "We don't deserve to be treated this way. Everyone, even that ignorant lawyer lady, Payton, is quick to say they don't have any concerns about Jade staying in our home, at least not as a foster child."

"Is the evaluation the last hurdle?"

"I hope so," Mandi sighed. "We are reaching the end of our rope. It's getting hard to continue to be gracious to the people we have to deal with there. Every time we hear from anyone at the Division or see our attorney's number flash on our caller IDs, we cringe."

"Hey, I have to go," Kelsey said suddenly. "I'll call you back in a little while."

"Sure, no problem."

While understandable—Mandi assumed someone had walked into her friend's office—, Kelsey's abrupt termination of the call left her with a mind swirling in uneasy, helpless thoughts. She stared at the bedroom wall as they ran through her head.

Justin and I have done nothing wrong.

We are paying a small fortune to defend ourselves when no one has yet to level a valid complaint about our current lives, home or family as it applies to Jade's well-being. Or to anyone's well-being for that matter.

We have even been acknowledged as compassionate, productive members of society, our accomplishments previously celebrated by the same agencies now unwilling to acknowledge any of it.

Despite nothing in my present life indicating that my past is an issue, these people are digging up skeletons I tucked away half a lifetime ago.

These people are picking at scabs long healed over until blood gushes out of them, at which point they walk away—curiosity satisfied—as I scramble, once again, to attempt to contain the damage.

My family and I are being hunted, threatened, tormented and I can't stop them,

—I can't stop it—,

because these people have the fate of our daughter in their ignorant hands. We have to take it,

—how much longer can we be expected to take it—

even though it might all be for nothing, even though we might still lose her in the end.

I have to pretend it doesn't hurt,

we have to—

Before Mandi completely realized what she was doing, she had leapt off the bed, grabbed a statue of a woman stretching toward the sky from the nightstand and flung it at the wall with a frustrated scream. It gave easily as the statue crashed into it before tumbling to the bed.

Mandi looked at the gaping hole, a clear view behind the drywall—

I knew this house was never properly insulated.

—before turning and walking out. She found her way to the living room and sat on the couch.

It was unusual for her to react so physically. In fact, had Justin or the kids done anything similar it would have no doubt triggered from her a stern lecture about appreciating the value of the things their family works hard for.

My apparent hypocrisy is something I can now tuck myself into bed under each night, she thought dryly.

Mandi sighed, rubbing her temples and leaning back against the couch to stare up at the ceiling. Most people would raise their eyebrows or gasp at the wall, some—she knew—would even withdraw in horror, but she wasn't so shocked.

What most didn't realize was that their family had been sustaining tremendous blows for nearly half a year now. They were attacks unforeseen; assaults which remained unjustifiable yet left them with little defense or recourse just the same. They simply had to keep standing despite the onslaught. Consequently, it wasn't entirely unfathomable to Mandi that their home now also bore similar damage.

Their battles weren't the sum of them any more than that hole was the sum of the house, but certainly—as Mandi sat there studying the light fixtures—it did raise the question of how much any entity could expect to withstand before it crumbled. They loved Jade as their own. They were willing to fight to the death for her, yet standing at the brink...

Is that really a practical reality for the one child who is stuck with us no matter what happens with Jade? For us? Even, really, for Jade?

It was a dark, bewildering place. One Mandi would have preferred never to have discovered.

"How would you rate your level of anxiety these days?"

Though the question was directed at Mandi, both she and Justin laughed. The psychologist seemed to get the humor in the question and clarified, "I mean, other than this adoption business."

"The adoption has been going on so long, it's hard to remember," Mandi answered truthfully, "but, in general, it really takes quite a bit to get me anxious. I don't think it's any higher than what would be considered normal. I've never felt it was unreasonable given the circumstances."

Turning to Justin, the doctor asked, "Do you ever find that Mandi worries about things which seem odd to you?"

"No, not at all," Justin replied, then paused before adding thoughtfully, "except—,"

Mandi almost fell out of her chair. *Did he just say "except"?* She noticed the doctor's attention piqued as well.

"—you know, like the same stuff the guys at work talk about their wives or girlfriends worrying about; stuff none of us really understand what the big deal is. So I guess I'm saying I don't always understand her concerns, but they seem to be in line with what..." Justin's voice trailed off as he cast a cautious glance sideways at Mandi.

"With what the opposite gender typically concerns itself with?" Dr. Castle offered.

Justin laughed, "Right."

Rolling her eyes genially, relieved Justin had not lost his mind as she originally feared, Mandi said, "He leaves his socks everywhere.

Baby Girl

For days—"

"—so she throws them away," Justin finished indignantly, but not without a hint of humor.

The doctor raised his eyebrows, entertained by the glimpse into their lives. He was an older, large man whose jovial nature didn't quite disguise his keen intelligence. His office was peppered with literature on a variety of topics related to forensic psychology.

"He was given fair warning," Mandi retorted casually, looking at Justin and waving her hand dismissively, "and, besides, he has hundreds of socks. Literally hundreds. I don't think he's thrown a sock away since high school." As if it just occurred to her, Mandi turned to him inquisitively, "Who keeps buying you all those socks anyway?"

Grinning, Justin ignored her question.

"Anyway," she continued with her explanation, "Throwing them away is a much less stressful solution for us both than me nagging him about it."

"It's not really a problem we have anymore," Justin admitted soberly.

With a triumphant wave of her hand, Mandi asserted, "See?"

The doctor laughed, "Well, exploring that would likely take another therapy session entirely, specifically, Justin, why it sounds as if you are incapable of being re-trained like most men. It took my wife a couple of years, but she had me under control after that. You must be especially stubborn if it's come to this."

Mandi and Justin laughed, grateful his laid back personality was making an otherwise undesirable situation more bearable.

"Okay, now," he continued, becoming serious once again, looking back at Mandi, "how do you handle loss?"

She thought about it, "Well, I guess it depends on what the loss is and how significant. If it's something big, I get sad, sometimes angry, but I'm typically very adept at finding my way to the other side. I am notoriously good at seeing the bright side to almost every situation... it might just take me a second to get up if it's bad enough that it really knocked me on my butt."

"How long is a second?"

Uncertain how to answer—*Is there a right answer here?*—, Mandi shrugged and tried to be honest. "It depends on the incident. Most things I recover from fairly quickly. At least functionally. I might still be sad, but it is seldom pervasive beyond the initial shock. I—We—have a really good life. What we are facing right now with this adoption is one of the most traumatic and heart-wrenching things either of us has ever experienced as adults. We are trying to do it right, but it is a struggle and I'm sure we don't always succeed."

"Yeah, that's no joke," Justin spoke up. "You know, I think just the fact Mandi has held it together so well through this whole ordeal—under tremendous strain—is proof that she can handle whatever issues arose during the time of her mother's death as a teenager, not to mention everything since. If anything, those moments have only made her stronger."

He hasn't seen the wall, Mandi thought regretfully.

Somehow she doubted it would change his mind, as he had seen more moments of her carrying the stress well than not, yet that hole was enough to plant a seed of misgiving in her own mind. There was no way to deny that things had been getting more difficult lately. The stress was wearing on both of them.

Part of Mandi knew that any reasonable person, having been put through what they had steadily endured for months now, would have a moment or two of pounding fists against the sidewalk in frustration.

Baby Girl

She also knew that any psychologist worth their weight would tell her negative emotions are a normal and healthy part of the human experience. They were, after all, talking about the future of the little girl—now more than a year old—they had loved and watched thrive since her fifteenth day of life. If Mandi or Justin could be complacent about the possibility of losing her, then something would certainly be wrong with that as well.

Still.

Mandi didn't like that she'd gotten so upset. It made her wonder if the psychological evaluation might expose something unanticipated.

Is there any way such a test can tell if a person is legitimately crazy versus simply being driven crazy by their current, temporary circumstances? If not, and the test shows I am under incredible strain, will we have an opportunity to make that case to the commissioner? Or will he just look at the report and move Jade immediately? After I insisted on this road through my initial determination to bring Jade into our home, am I now the one who will cost us everything?

The pressure was unbelievable; the stakes inconceivable.

"I will be honest," the doctor confided, "given what I've read so far about this case, in addition to talking with you both, I believe this to be much ado about nothing. The written tests will tell us for sure, but this seems more like a hoop the court is making you jump through in order to be certain there are no lingering issues than the sincere suspicion of a problem."

Mandi and Justin nodded.

"I have no doubt it causes apprehension despite that," he continued, "but be grateful that at least we live in a country with a legitimate process for adopting children. In some countries, getting a baby is nothing more than sliding five-or-so thousand dollars to a judge and leaving with the child."

"Find me that judge," Justin joked.

Mandi laughed. She knew what the doctor meant—such a system obviously didn't protect its children from those who prey on the youngest of humanity—and was certain Justin did as well, but she also understood his remark. In this case, already at five or six times that amount in legal fees despite having no substantiated complaints of neglect or abuse against them, the other approach did seem at least a little appealing.

The doctor grinned good-naturedly, unaffected by the quip. He knew the two in front of him had been through quite a bit.

"Alright, Mandi," he finished up, "all we have left is for you to take the written tests. Do you have time now?"

"Sure," she responded. "I've taken the day off, so we might as well go ahead and get it done."

"Great," he said enthusiastically, "just remember to answer truthfully—typically the first answer that comes to your head is the best one—and be careful not to over think any of the questions. Sometimes smarter people tend to do that and then end up with inconsistent or invalid test results."

"Okay, no problem," she replied, though she truly had no idea if it would be a problem or not.

Over thinking things can sometimes be a specialty of mine.

"It will take time to analyze the results," Dr. Castle advised them, "but I should be able to get back to your attorney with my findings in a week or two."

Mandi and Justin nodded.

"Alright, then," he rose from his chair, "if you'll follow me to the other room, Mandi, my assistant will get you all set up."

T or F: I think it would be exciting to be a forest fire fighter.

Mandi blinked. It had to be the fifth question about fighting forest fires she had come across and, despite the doctor's advice, her analytical mind couldn't help but try to decipher what the connection might be. She shook her head.

Move On.

Mandi thought fighting forest fires would no doubt be exciting in the not-boring-in-the-midst-of-it way, but not so much in the can't-wait-to-get-to-my-favorite-vacation-spot way. Two different definitions of excitement and it wasn't entirely clear which they meant. She opted for the latter.

False.

T or F: I like talking about sex.

Christ.

In truth, the subject wasn't one Mandi felt any aversion to. Certainly, she could further qualify the statement to exclude most relatives and colleagues, but the question didn't provide any such context. In its absence, it didn't seem to take much of a leap to see how either answer could be misconstrued. Interpreted by someone very conservative, true might be viewed quite negatively. Yet the alternative might suggest she held some unhealthy view of a natural function of human existence.

True.

T or F: I find it frustrating when another's incompetence holds up a project I am working on.

It was too true to warrant additional thought, though she was aware it might not paint her as the most patient or tolerant individual.

True.

T or F: I feel as if people are watching me.

Mandi looked around. There was no one else in the room. The receptionist visible through the open door was typing at her computer, but glanced up as if she sensed Mandi looking at her.

Now is not the time for jokes.

False.

Sighing, Mandi looked at the numbers on the three answer sheets in front of her, quickly doing the math.

Only 894 more to go.

13 – Day 385

"Turn on the news," Justin said as soon as Mandi answered her phone.

"What—"

"Channel nine," he cut her off impatiently, urging, "hurry!"

Jumping up from her desk, Mandi grabbed the remote and pointed it at the television. It flickered on, already set to the station he was referencing. She waited for the sound to come on, watching the monitor curiously in the interim.

"Is it on?" Justin asked.

"Yeah, watching," she responded.

He fell silent.

On the screen in front of her was a picture of a red-haired boy who appeared to be no more than seven, with a pale complexion and freckles. He was cute despite the dark circles under his eyes, his sunken cheeks and the wariness with which he seemed to be looking at whoever had snapped the photograph.

The voice of the anchor faded in, "... *authorities believe Sebastian has endured the abuse since his father got remarried. He allegedly spent most of his time locked in a make-shift cage in the basement of the family home. Having minimal access to food or water, he resorted to eating the cardboard* on the floor where he was kept. When he went to the bathroom inside the enclosure, as he was sometimes confined to it for twenty-four hour periods, he was beaten and ridiculed."

Mandi gasped.

Hearing her through the phone, Justin said grimly, "It gets even more unbelievable."

"*A neighbor called the abuse hotline out of concern for the boy after what he described as suspicious behavior by the parents, never seeing the child leave the house, and hearing frequent shouting. Child Protective Services visited the home twice, conducting an interview with the parents and child, finding no cause for concern. –* "

Gasping again, Mandi asked, "Anderson County?"

"Yep," Justin confirmed dryly.

"*– Realizing nothing was being done to help the boy, convinced something was amiss, the neighbor waited until he saw the parents leave the house, then entered the residence through a back door he was aware they kept unlocked. Finding the boy locked in the basement, surrounded by chicken wire, he called the police. Authorities tonight have both parents in custody, while the child has been placed with Child Protective Services.*

"*We attempted to reach out to Anderson County CPS for a comment on this story, but have not heard back as of the time of this airing.*

"*In other news...*"

Mandi turned away from the television in disbelief.

"Can you believe that?" Justin asked incredulously.

"No, I can't," she responded, shaking her head.

"They said at the beginning that the Division conducted a single telephone interview, then two interviews at the house, both of which they scheduled in advance," he told her.

"Idiots," Mandi shook her head.

"I feel bad for that little boy," Justin went on. "I'm not trying to take anything away from his situation. It's just that after… you know after everything the Division has put us through… it seems especially offensive."

"Yeah, absolutely," Mandi agreed. "I know exactly what you're saying. At times I have tried to tell myself they are just being especially diligent with the children in their care and they deserve respect for that, no matter how inconvenient it is in our case. This though, along with the nonsensical nature of our ongoing battle, makes me wonder if the kids are even really a priority."

"Exactly. The couple was married," Justin pointed out sarcastically. "You think that was a factor?"

Mandi pressed her fingers into the bridge of her nose, willing away the stress headache. She still did not want to believe they — or even that helpless little boy — were at the mercy of such a simplistic and short-sighted system or the people it employed. That any worker could walk into a home, see a boy looking like the one in the picture just displayed, and not react with at least twice the vigor and indignation they did in response to the healthy, happy little girl that was Jade… It was unfathomable.

Is it really the lack of marriage working against us? Is it that our success in other areas causes resentment? Is it truly some political battle that has no concern for the individual circumstances or people involved? People too overworked to recognize problems from solutions, friends from enemies? Whatever it was that was supposed to help these kids, to save these littlest of people, it missed Sebastian — the exact type of child it was designed to protect — by a country mile.

"It's just wrong on so many levels," Mandi finally said. "I don't understand how an agency with such good intentions can miss its mark so completely with both Jade and Sebastian."

Justin agreed, "It's like they inverted what their mission is supposed to be. Coming after Jade and leaving that boy in those conditions. It's horrible."

"Thank goodness that neighbor was willing to get involved and take such a big risk," Mandi shook her head again. "It just goes to show that putting one's head down assuming someone else will handle whatever is wrong in the world doesn't always work. Who knows how much longer that kid would have suffered if he hadn't done what he did?"

"Before I called you, they said police think he'd been living like that for six-to-eight months. You're right; it could have gone on much longer."

Mandi sighed into the phone, "Yeah."

"Well, I have to get back to this training class. We just had a break and I happened to catch the news while I was standing in the cafeteria."

"Sure," Mandi nodded.

"It just makes me sick," he explained. "I understand this less and less with every passing day. I guess I always took for granted that there were agencies taking care of these children, that while they might not be perfect, they were at least adept at recognizing the adversary. And I sure as heck thought it would take a lot more than anything we ever did and a lot less than what Sebastian's parents did for them to identify that."

"I know," she responded, turning off the TV and walking back to her desk, sitting down in front of the computer. "I assumed a lot of things as well, but now I think I just wasn't involved, wasn't paying attention. I am guessing most people aren't, most people are just like we were."

"There isn't anyone I've talked to about this who isn't surprised," Justin mentioned. After a slight pause, he exclaimed, "Oh that reminds me! Have you checked your email recently? I forwarded you the reference letter from Blake and his fiancé. I scanned it in so we can keep the original copy."

"I haven't had a chance since I put the kids in bed," Mandi responded, "but I will check as soon as we hang up."

Kendal had requested they collect a list of references to include with the results of the psychological evaluation. He felt the commissioner didn't buy into the arguments of the Guardian ad Litem, but still wanted to make certain there was ample evidence supporting a decision in their favor should something go 'wrong' down the road.

"He did a really thorough job with it. I was really surprised! I think Lacey must have helped him."

"Well, definitely be sure to thank them for me as well."

Once Mandi finished the call with Justin, she clicked over to her email. As promised, the reference letter was waiting. Scanning the page-long document, she thought, *He was right; they didn't spare any effort on this.*

It made her feel good to know so many of their friends and family were standing with them through all of this. Justin and she — in particular — had always been relatively independent people, typically the ones others leaned on rather than the ones doing the leaning. That had not been the case as much recently. She was learning, however, that while it might not feel natural or comfortable needing to borrow the strength of others on occasion, it was definitely a gift to discover so many willing to lend it to them.

Mandi printed out the last reference letter they had been waiting for and added it to the stack of others, all ready to be handed to

Kendal at their next status meeting.

Non-relative Reference
RE: Mandi Williams, Justin Rice

To Whom It May Concern:

My name is Blake Evans and my fiancé and I are writing this letter of recommendation on behalf of our good friends Justin and Mandi in the matter of their pending adoption. We have known Justin and Mandi for the past three years and have come to know what amazing and caring people they are.

As we are planning on having a family of our own, we can't think of better role models for our future children to grow up around. They are always doing activities with Matthew and seem to have the perfect balance of love and discipline that shows in what a lovely boy he is. A perfect example of this would be the time we spent the entire day enjoying the Indy Races at the Speedway with Justin, Mandi and Matthew. Justin and Mandi both worked together to make sure Matthew had the time of his life. Also, at the same time making sure Matthew was well behaved and polite to everyone he came in contact with.

In the time we have been friends it is plain to see their children are the light of their lives. We truly believe that Jade couldn't be with better parents than Justin and Mandi and it is easy to see how their love has grown for her during their time together. Whenever they talk about their future it always includes their hopes and dreams for their children and how their lives will continue to grow together.

If anyone is in a position to adopt a child it is Justin and Mandi. They truly deserve to be parents and give all of themselves to raising healthy happy kids. It is our hope and prayer that the desires of their hearts are met and they are blessed with the opportunity to have Jade in their lives forever.

Sincerely,

Blake Evans,
Lacey Howard

Baby Girl

Non-relative Reference
RE: Mandi Williams, Justin Rice

To Whom It May Concern:

I have known Mandi Williams and Justin Rice for about ten years. In that time I have found Mandi to be a fierce and loving advocate for her children and a dependable friend. Justin and Mandi have complementary parenting styles that provide a centered and balanced family life for their children. Between them they provide the structure and discipline kids need and the safety and love kids crave. I would never hesitate to leave my child in their care and I can't imagine a better home for the baby they have cared for and loved for over a year. Mandi and Justin have a strong support network of family and friends they can turn to in times of need and they work hard to provide for all the family's physical and emotional needs.

Please feel free to contact me with any questions.

Kelsey Carson

Daycare\School Reference
RE: Mandi Williams, Justin Rice

To Whom It May Concern:

We are writing this letter in support of Mandi Williams and Justin Rice. We have had the wonderful opportunity of knowing these individuals for over two years and have been the childcare provider for their son, Matthew, as well as the foster children that have been in their care.

We have also had the pleasure to care for Baby Girl Reylco (Jade) while she has been in Mandi and Justin's care. We have been excited to see that they were given the opportunity to care for this wonderful baby girl. Before she was even old enough to attend our center they were doting parents and brought her in to meet our staff. For over a year now, we have watched Jade thrive in their care. They are such wonderful parents and have given this little girl a wonderful home. It is so amazing how much she loves her "Mommy" and "Daddy". She beams every time they come to pick her up!

Mandi and Justin have proven to be wonderful people and excellent parents. They are very involved in all of their children's lives, both biological and foster. Their parenting skills are over and beyond many parents that we experience. They are very open with their children and talk them through all the aspects of their developing lives. We are very pleased to be part of their lives and that they are part of ours. We stand by them in all of the parenting decisions they make and believe they are a very stable and wonderful family.

Thank you,

Deanna Randolph

Relative Reference
RE: Mandi Williams, Justin Rice

To Whom It May Concern:

We are grandparents to Justin and Mandi. Justin and Mandi and son, Matthew, have given "Baby Jade" their love and care. And all baby needs for an infant.

Jade was brought to them at fifteen days old. She has been a family member since. We have spent time at their home and witnessed the special care by both Justin and Mandi.

We love Jade and Matthew dearly!

Megan and Henry Rice

Relative Reference
RE: Mandi Williams, Justin Rice

To Whom It May Concern:

I am Justin Rice's great aunt. I know Justin to be honest, reliable and of high integrity. My husband, James, and I have spent time with Justin and Mandi, also visiting them in their home. They are loving, caring, fun and enjoyable. Family is of great importance in their lives.

Sincerely yours,
Lucy Santamaria

14 – Day 404

It happened twice in twenty-four hours.

The first time was as Mandi walked out of the grocery store the day before. She was replaying her last conversation with Sam's paralegal when she glanced to her left—to the east—and was surprised to see a bright rainbow stretching across the sky. Below it, a second, much lighter rainbow reflected off the clouds.

Mandi couldn't recall the last time she had seen a rainbow, which is why its sudden appearance surprised her. As a child, in a private Presbyterian school, she remembered being told rainbows were God's reminder that he wouldn't ever again give any of them more than they could withstand.

She found herself wishing she still believed in fairy tales.

The second time it happened was this morning. Mandi was making her way to meet Justin at the attorney's office, thinking with some angst about the situation involving Jade and the consultation ahead, of the fact they had yet to hear the outcome of the psychological evaluation which had occurred more than two weeks earlier. As she came to a stop at a light she discovered a bright rainbow stretched in front of her—to the west.

Though Mandi considered herself a more practical individual, one

Baby Girl

not predisposed toward a belief in signs or anything of such a fantastical nature, she had to admit to herself that it was harder to ignore the second time. Most likely it was nothing more than the fact everything surrounding the fight for Jade was simply making her more aware of the present, of the rainbows she had no doubt rushed past on many other days. Still, she couldn't deny how good it felt, given she had noticed both in the midst of pondering their very tenuous situation, to believe those rainbows might somehow be the universe trying to tell her that it would all turn out right in the end.

For a moment—just a moment—her mind fully entertained the possibility of a world where everything happened for the best at just in time.

It is hope. Real or imagined, I will take it.

The meeting with Kendal had been somewhat sober. He hadn't heard back from the psychologist yet—though he reiterated his certainty that Mandi had done well—but he wanted to discuss with them what the next steps would be once he had the report in hand. Although a positive psychological evaluation would be a major blow to whatever case Payton was trying to put together, Mandi and Justin were disappointed to hear that Sam didn't expect her to back off completely.

After the solemn visit, the two made their way to the parking garage.

"Oh!" Justin exclaimed as they were about to head opposite directions, "I have a kind of interesting story to tell you. I will have to share it with you this evening."

"Tell me now," Mandi suggested as they came to a stop on the sidewalk. She was eager for any story that might distract from the heaviness of the conversation they had just had.

"Well, earlier today I got everything I needed to done at work and started thinking about all the stuff coming up with Jade, so I couldn't concentrate on anything new—"

Mandi nodded knowingly, "Uh-huh..."

"Well, I was walking around the parts warehouse, literally doing little more than reading part numbers."

"Okay."

"I came to a stop, still thinking about things—all thoughts centered around Jade, the meeting with Kendal, how much longer we might have to go through this nonsense, if it's going to be enough in the end—and looked down at the floor to discover this..."

Reaching into his pocket, Justin pulled out a small blue stone. Mandi looked curiously at his outstretched hand. The stone had the word *Hope* engraved on one side.

"Wow," Mandi said, eyes widening, a laugh of disbelief escaping her lips, "that's really cool."

Justin nodded, smiling, "I took it as maybe a good sign."

"Definitely," she agreed, going on to tell him, "especially since when I picked Jade up from the hospital someone acquainted with her biological family—either her mother, other family or a friend of theirs—left her a small stone with a guardian angel embedded in it. It's about the same size as this one actually. Did I ever show it to you?"

Surprised, Justin shook his head, though he acknowledged sheepishly, "You might have. I'm not sure the significance would have registered with me at the time."

Mandi grinned, "Yeah, I have it with her stuff from the hospital. I've tucked it into my pocket for good luck more than once as we've navigated all this."

Baby Girl

Justin looked down at the stone in his hand, commenting thoughtfully, "Maybe it really is a sign then."

"I sure hope so," Mandi remarked, thinking of the rainbows she hadn't known how to tell him about without sounding silly.

Maybe it's not silly after all. Maybe it's just a way of dealing.

Jade toddled up behind Mandi as she was vacuuming the carpet by the back door in the kitchen.

"Up, up, up," she said urgently, thrusting her arms toward the ceiling with each word to emphasize her meaning. While Jade wasn't exactly scared of the vacuum cleaner, her preference was to be in the arms of whoever was operating it.

Reaching down, Mandi wrapped one arm around the little girl's waist, hauling her up until she was comfortably settled on Mandi's hip. She continued to vacuum with her free hand.

They had just arrived home from work and daycare. Justin was on his way to meet some friends for the evening, while Mandi had decided to get a bit of quick cleaning done before starting supper.

Having seen the exchange with Jade, Matthew ran to get his favorite bear, Stitches. Upon returning to the kitchen a few seconds later, he exclaimed, "Here you go, Jade! Now you don't have to be scared because Stitches will protect you."

Leaning forward from Mandi's arm, Jade reached for the stuffed animal. Eagerly, she pulled it to her chest with both arms as she returned to her original position. She looked at Matthew, then Mandi, then squealed wide-eyed in sheer delight.

Mandi smiled. "That's a great job looking out for sissy," she told Matthew. "You are an excellent big brother."

"I used to be scared of the vacuum cleaner too," the four-year-old informed her with a casual shrug, turning to leave the room, "then I grew out of it because I got bigger, but Stitches helped me until then. He will help her too."

Seeing Matthew depart, Jade squirmed to be let down—"Down, down, down"—then followed after him, toting his bear by the arm.

Mandi resumed vacuuming.

Even if they can't acknowledge the reality of Jade's bond with Justin and me, they wouldn't be able to deny how strong it is between her and Matthew. If they would only take the time to visit they would see she has a brother and he has a sister. Simple as that.

I hope I never have to explain to him why she's no longer here.

Mandi's thoughts were interrupted by her phone's audible notification of a new text message.

Justin Rice: I just heard a song that is a favorite of mine. Havent heard it n years. Hope it a good sign. It called "meant to be together"
Sent: 5:44PM

Mandi felt tears burn her eyes at the optimistic message.

She, Justin, Matthew and Jade would always share this history, irrespective of whatever the future might hold. Perhaps only she and Justin would be able to remember it clearly—*perhaps that is ultimately for the best*—, but at their core the four of them were tied together in a way no court had jurisdiction over. They had walked this path together. While the road forward had yet to be determined, no one could ever erase the footsteps of where they had been.

Hope.

Mandi was encouraged that Justin had found it too. On this day and at this point in their journey, it was worth everything.

Sam Kendal was sitting at his desk, working late when the phone rang. The receptionist had left for the night, so he reached for the phone himself.

"Hello?"

"Samuel Kendal, please," the female voice requested cordially.

"This is he."

"Mr. Kendal, my name is Shauna Dean. I work with Darren Castle. You retained his services for your clients, Mandi Williams and Justin Rice."

"Yes, Ms. Dean," he responded in recognition. "That's correct. How may I help you?"

"Dr. Castle requested that I confirm your email address before forwarding you an official letter with his findings on Mr. Rice and Ms. Williams."

"Of course, that will be great," Sam said with satisfaction, happy to hear the news. "We have been waiting for his report."

After confirming the address, she said, "Okay, it should be on its way. If you have any questions about the evaluation, Dr. Castle said to feel free to contact him. He is prepared to go to the hearing if necessary. Please give me a call back if you don't receive the email or if you experience any trouble with the attachment."

"I already see it in my inbox," he confirmed cheerfully. "Thank you very much."

"No problem. Have a nice night."

"You too."

Hanging up the office phone, Sam smiled as he opened and started reading the letter from the psychologist.

Juli L. Idleman

Castle & Associates
Specialists in Forensic Psychology

Darren J. Castle, Ph.D.
Steven Green, Ph.D.
Licensed Psychologists

RE: MANDI WILLIAMS EVALUATION

Dear Mr. Kendal:

In regard to her candidacy for adoption of Baby Girl Reylco, you referred Mandi Williams to our office for an assessment of her mental health status. As is standard protocol with these evaluations, I interviewed Ms. Williams, age 30, and her partner, Justin Rice, age 35. Subsequent to the interview, Ms. Williams also completed the following psychological tests:

>Personality Research Form-E (measuring normal Personality traits)

>Minnesota Multiphasic Personality Inventory-2 (measuring dimensions of potential emotional instability, problem behavioral patterns, and symptoms of diagnosable mental illnesses)

>Child Abuse Potential Inventory (measuring likelihood of abusive acting out toward children)

Lastly, I reviewed the reports prepared by the licensing manager with Child Protective Services, the independent adoptive home study and the textual summary of the grievance request made by Ms. Williams and Mr. Rice.

In the course of my appraisal, including my review of the documents, my testing and my clinical interview, I paid particular attention to Ms. Williams' own childhood background, including the loss of her mother, and the effect of those early experiences on her current mental health performance and potential for healthy parenting.

Findings

Ms. Williams was forthcoming and credible in her clinical interview, describing her stress reactions as a teen and how she benefited from mental health services in those early weeks and months after her mother's death. She is currently experiencing no mental health symptoms worthy of treatment, and she has not needed or taken psychiatric medications since she was a teen.

She rarely drinks alcohol, and she has never used illegal drugs. Her stress outlets include exercise, spending time with her family, building things such as model planes, and studying Buddhism. She expressed a passion for learning new things. Her partner Mr. Rice stated that Ms. Williams is managing her normal situational life stresses very well.

The results from Ms. Williams psychological testing can be considered valid, as her answers were found to be open and non-distorting.

Ms. Williams' testing results point toward a normal, mentally fit individual with no indications of diagnosable mental health disorders or symptoms, including impulsivity, hostility, thought disorder, depression, anxiety, antisocial tendencies or potential for child abuse. Ms. Williams appears in her testing to be an assertive, serious, cautious, open, modest individual who is extremely resilient and socially accountable.

Conclusion

It is my determination, the aforementioned process serving as evidence, that Ms. Williams is a normal, psychologically healthy individual with no mental health symptoms and no need for psychological treatment. I have every reason to believe that she is an outstanding parent and an exceptional candidate for adoption.

Respectfully,

Darren C. Castle, Ph.D.
Licensed Psychologist

Sam wouldn't have taken on the Williams-Rice case if his initial impression of Mandi and Justin hadn't been favorable. There simply wasn't enough money anyone could ever offer to convince him to fight for a placement he truly believed was in opposition to a child's best interests. Fortunately, every conversation since the first one with them had continued to deepen his conviction that these were indeed the intelligent, sincere, balanced people they represented themselves to be.

It's still reassuring to have an independent, third party corroborate that belief.

He forwarded the attachment to Mandi. It was after work hours for most, but he knew she often checked email once the kids went to bed.

Mandi:

I have attached Dr. Castle's report. It is very favorable.

Sam

Despite the casual tone of his message, Sam had not missed the concern Mandi and Justin expressed—both explicit and implicit—during their meeting earlier in the day. It was evident they were worried the length of time it was taking Castle to issue his findings might be indicative of something negative.

Sam smiled to himself as he clicked send, then shut down his computer to head home for the evening.

The report is a good note to end the day on.

He was confident he had just made one very determined, yet very exhausted, family's night.

15 – Day 421

Mandi Williams: Welcome to the six month anniversary of one of the worst days of our lives. Congratulations on still having Jade 183 days later!
Sent: 9:17AM

Justin Rice: Wow. I didn't realize it had been that long. Time flies when you're fighting for your kid!
Sent: 9:20AM

"This doesn't change anything," Edith stated as she finished reading the mental health evaluation on Mandi Williams, tossing it down on her desk.

Payton grimaced. *Of course not.*

After avoiding Sam's phone calls for almost two weeks, she had received the evaluation via certified mail that morning, along with a note that Sam wanted to speak with her at her earliest convenience. She had copied the letter from Dr. Castle and placed it on Edith's desk.

"It doesn't?" Payton asked with a sigh.

"It sure as hell doesn't," Edith snapped. "They paid off a psychologist. So what? That doesn't mean we just roll on this deal!"

"Edith," she implored, feeling a little desperate—after all she was the one who had to show up in court to face the disbelieving looks of everyone in the room; the fit she'd had to throw at the last hearing in order to gum it up had been humiliating—, "Baby Girl is well over a year old now. This is the family she's been with since she was a newborn. Every step of the way, every hurdle we have thrown up—the staffing, appealing the grievance, the Nelsons refusing to back down, the questions of mental health—they have managed to overcome. To be honest, this is starting to feel…" her voice trailed off uncomfortably.

"Feel what?" Edith challenged.

"Vindictive," Payton tried. "A little too much about us and not so much about them."

"We agreed there was no way a family lacking the traditional stability necessary to raise a child would be allowed—"

"No," Payton corrected, cutting her off, "you said there was no way that would happen and I went along with it."

"And now you think I'm wrong?" Edith snarled in contempt.

"Now I think it's getting a little old," she responded evenly. "I truly have no idea what else we can claim to take issue with. Edith, they have more than proven their devotion to this child, regardless of their marital status or whatever happens in their personal relationship in the future. I don't honestly have any doubt remaining that both of them will always be there for her. I mean, do you really think they would go through all of this and not be?"

Ignoring the question, Edith posed one of her own, "What did you tell their attorney about this latest development?"

Sighing, sensing defeat, Payton answered with resignation, "I have been avoiding speaking to him, but I'm not going to be able to much longer. I know he likely wants me to agree to put this on the uncontested docket and drop any opposition."

"That's not going to happen," Edith declared obdurately. "They're trying to make fools of us, Payton!"

Grimacing, she said, dismay etched on her every feature, "I honestly think they just want their daughter."

"She isn't their daughter!" Edith all but yelled. "They had no right to do what they did and they still have no right! They are *just* foster parents. They don't get to decide what's best for the children placed with them. That's *our* job!"

Payton didn't say anything, only stared at her colleague.

Exasperated, Edith directed, "If you can't find fault with the couple, then go after the staffing itself. Tell the commissioner it was two people in a room that overturned a staffing containing twelve people. What kind of procedure is that?"

Shaking her head, Payton responded half-heartedly, "I don't know..."

"It's one shaky step from chaos is what it is! Go back to our first plan after the staffing was initially overturned. Tell the commissioner you believe a second staffing should be held, as it's likely the next one will find more suitable parents, just as the first one did.

"Once we get another staffing, I will demolish every chance this couple has of keeping that girl and any other child placed in their care! I obviously underestimated them originally, I admit, but it won't happen again. If we can't outright beat them, all we have to do is hold on longer than they can."

"Edith..." Payton shook her head, disbelief creeping into her voice, "is this really because they aren't married?"

"I-It's the principle of it, Payton," Edith sputtered, caught off guard. "The principle!" Recovering herself, she added, "And I guarantee you they don't have the resources to fight this thing forever."

"I don't know," she hesitated.

Edith sounded almost maniacal, not simply unwilling but possibly unable to look at things logically. Watching her, Payton found herself wondering, *Am I as bad as her for not stopping this?*

"I do," Edith said with conviction. After a moment, a look of excitement crossed her face. "In fact, that lawyer of theirs is one of the most expensive adoption attorneys this side of the state. I bet if we drag this thing out long enough we can demand new financial statements and use any debt they've incurred fighting this battle to further question whether they have adequate means to support Baby Girl!"

Payton cringed. It was the Kassie incident all over again. *This isn't why I accepted a pay cut to get out of corporate law.*

"Doesn't this feel," she tried again, "a little too personal? I mean, in the beginning, maybe there was some cause for legitimate concern or further investigation, but don't you think—"

"No, Payton, it doesn't and I don't!" Edith cut her off furiously. "Unless you want to take this matter up with our director, your job is to support the recommendations I make at the staffings! You need to call that attorney and let him know this case will *not* be on the uncontested docket."

Payton sighed.

While Edith's statement wasn't entirely true—their job was actually to represent the interests of the child, not run their own agenda—she had given up fighting this woman long ago. Although she was growing tired of dealing with the fallout, it didn't make any sense to start trying to change things now. She sure didn't want to

Baby Girl

drag anything in front of the director, where Edith might have a chance to exercise her political connections, a game she had no doubt perfected far better than Payton.

"They're the ones who are in the wrong," Edith went on vehemently, as if reciting a mantra. "They had *no* right to go against the original staffing. They had *no* right to presume they had ultimate say in what is best for that child. They are *not* her parents.

"You are a good person so of course you feel bad they have gone through so much, but you need to remember they brought it all on themselves. They should have been gracious and trusted the outcome of the original staffing. Can you imagine a world where every foster family conducted themselves with the gumption of these two? We have an obligation, Payton," she stated with self-righteous resentment, "an *obligation* to make certain this family doesn't set some sort of precedent!"

"Fine, Edith," Payton sighed. She just wanted the woman to stop talking.

"What does fine mean?"

"It means I will call Sam Kendal later today to advise him this needs to stay on the contested docket."

"I think that will be best," Edith visibly relaxed once she saw Payton was going to do as she wished. "Thank you."

"My clients are willing to meet with you," Sam told her, perplexed. "Don't you think it might make more sense to convene with them and Jade before taking this stance? My understanding is that you've never even sat down with them."

"That's not the issue," Payton told him, frustrated. She had attempted to inform him of the decision to keep the adoption hearing on the contested docket despite the assessment, only to find herself bombarded with questions.

Sam was typically a patient man. His many years of law and dealing with CPS had taught him that it was always best to try to appeal to an opponent's good reason and common sense before becoming antagonistic. Using this method, nine-times-out-of-ten a case could be settled without requiring an aggressive battle, which was costly and inevitably raised the stakes for both sides. The odds of success were always decreased when an amicable agreement couldn't be reached, if only because it required the introduction of a third party—the commissioner or judge—along with all of their individual biases and quirks.

Despite that knowledge, Payton was testing his commitment to the pacifist approach.

"Hello?" Payton asked impatiently.

"I'm here," Sam said. "I'm just trying to figure out what the issue is. I would prefer we resolve whatever questions you have before we get in front of the commissioner if that's at all possible. As you are likely aware, a contested hearing will prove costly and time-consuming for both sides."

"There is nothing you or your clients can clear up," Payton replied curtly. "Our issue is with the original staffing being overturned."

Sam was too dumbfounded to speak.

How can meeting with my clients not be applicable to the outcome of the original staffing or the reasons why it was overturned?

"I will want to put on just one witness, I think, from the Children's Division," Payton pushed forward, uncomfortable with his silence, "involved in this case. I will take a look and give you the name of the worker. I will try to do that in the next week or two in the event you want to do any discovery before the hearing."

"I would appreciate it," Sam answered courteously, falling back to his polite demeanor while he struggled to figure out what this woman's true complaint could possibly be.

"However, I believe you know the evidence we have. The reasons your clients were not chosen in the beginning are the reasons our office doesn't support them in their adoption petition."

"Have you reviewed those reasons?" Sam couldn't help but ask, though he tried to sound kind rather than condescending.

"I have," she snapped defensively.

"Have you heard how those reasons were addressed during the grievance that overturned it? How they were found to either be inapplicable or completely false?"

"The Division did not make available to us a detailed response to each reason—"

"My office would be happy to supply you that," Sam offered, for what he knew wasn't the first time.

"That's not necessary," she answered shortly.

Not necessary?

Sam kept his thoughts to himself. He didn't want to aggravate Payton any further. It was obvious she was already tense. As contemptibly lazy as he found her, he didn't want to motivate her into attempting to move Jade from the Williams-Rice home out of spite either.

When Sam didn't respond, Payton cleared her throat and continued, "We feel the Division ought to recruit for better families. Certainly those involved in the staffing felt there were other, better ones for this child at that time and nothing has really changed as far as those facts and circumstances. So, to put it simply, our position is that some further recruitment will probably bring about other more suitable resources for this child, just as it did on the first occasion."

Sam didn't respond. None of the things he wanted to say would be appropriate or helpful.

"It should not take me long to bring this evidence forward. I would like to know if you intend to put on any witnesses besides your clients and, of course, your cross examination of my witness."

"I will have to give it some thought," Sam said carefully, "but I am certainly also willing to share my list with you well in advance of the hearing. Fair enough?"

"Fair enough," she agreed, relieved he seemed to be backing off, at least for the moment.

"I know you are anxious to get this behind you," Sam sympathized when he called Mandi later in the day, "but I don't think it's in our best interest to rush this to court. I know I sound like a broken record, but every day Jade is with you is a day it becomes harder for the commissioner to justify—especially without any real good reason to begin with, which they obviously don't have—taking her from your home."

Mandi grimaced. She knew he was right, but two more months meant continued uncertainty, not to mention trying to hold their tongues during visits with the Division.

"There are a lot of really good people downtown," he went on, reminding himself as much as his client. "Unfortunately, as luck would have it, your case was assigned to one of the biggest buffoons they have."

"Oh my god, Mandi," Kelsey said during lunch, after having been filled in on the phone call from the adoption attorney. "This is absolutely crazy."

Mandi was still fuming. She told her friend, "I just... you would think if the Guardian ad Litem is so convinced we are unfit for Jade she wouldn't allow her to continue to be with us."

"Totally," Kelsey agreed, taking a bite of her sandwich. "We've talked about that before. None of this makes any sense. I can't believe they are getting away it."

"This Payton chick. She is fat and lazy and causing problems without ever having taken the time to get to know us or Jade so she can form her own opinion," Mandi stated with a disgusted growl of antipathy. She didn't often critique the appearance of others, but the level of contempt she felt for Payton was palpable and just as rare.

"She sounds absolutely dreadful," Kelsey commiserated, shaking her head.

"I can't believe she's basing her continued opposition of us on a staffing she wasn't even at for a child she has never met — a child and a family she *still* refuses to meet, by the way — and a grievance she hasn't even bothered to review in order to figure out if it does in fact invalidate the original staffing!"

Kelsey was alternating between shaking her head in loathing and nodding in agreement.

"The emotional, physical and financial cost her stupidity is causing us is staggering, not to mention positively infuriating!"

"Deep breaths, Mandi," Kelsey consoled. "Sanity must prevail."

"Yeah, but when?" she asked sincerely, shaking her head sadly, feeling helpless, "How much longer?"

Hoping she was right, Kelsey assured her, "Eventually."

16 – Day 436

They came into the room abruptly.

Lindsey Davis, Mandi's best friend from high school whom she hadn't spoken to since right after their daughter came to live with them, was being granted immediate custody of Jade. Mandi and Justin hadn't even been aware another family was still trying to adopt her, much less someone they knew.

Upset at being taken by people she didn't know, Jade screamed and reached for Mandi as they walked her out of the room.

She's gone.

Mandi tried to follow but felt paralyzed, sinking, her very breath knocked right out of her.

How can this be?

Insides aching, Mandi thought of Matthew, of him growing up as an only child after spending the last fourteen months as a big brother.

We can have more kids, but… no, we can't. Jade is our daughter. There will never be another Jade. This is it. We are done. If it can't be both Jade and Matthew, it will only be Matthew.

Mandi looked into the dark doorway of a room to her left. She knew Justin was in there, just as devastated as her. She wanted to comfort him, but couldn't think of anything comforting to say, so she

Baby Girl

remained immobile, unable to figure out what to do next.

Matthew and Jade are a set. This isn't right.

Maybe we can appeal.

The court's decision is final. There is no recourse remaining, no appeals left.

They were being engulfed by the vacuum of their worst fears and it was more terrible than anything Mandi could have ever imagined. The fight was over—the long days and nights of waiting and worrying were finally behind them—but instead of walking away with Jade, they were left with a gaping hole that could never be filled.

This isn't right. Jade is still here.

Mandi woke up forcefully.

Jade is still here.

Relief mixed with fading pain, her heart still pounding, Mandi glanced at the time. 2:48 AM.

Sam would be conducting witness interviews later in the day in preparation for their hearing next month. By the time he was done, they would know for certain who was on their side and who wasn't.

Rolling onto her back, Mandi looked up at the ceiling, feeling her heart start to settle down, her mind still awash in the negative emotions the dream had conjured.

Mandi had recently read that dreaming about or imagining a situation can evoke as strong an emotional and physical reaction as if the event had actually occurred. Biologically, the body knows no difference. That same book also mentioned that mental and physical pain share the same neural pathways, which is why mere psychological pain can sometimes feel as profoundly disabling as, for example, having one's arm sawed off.

I would give my arm, Mandi thought desperately. *It wouldn't be half as painful as losing one of my children.*

"Please state your name and your role with the Division," Sam requested, turning on the recording device.

"Dawn Cobbler," the young woman answered. "I am a caseworker."

"Specifically, you are the caseworker for Jad—er—Baby Girl Reylco?"

She nodded.

"Please speak your answers," he requested kindly, motioning to the recorder.

"Oh, sorry," Dawn giggled. "Yes, I am the current caseworker for Baby Girl Reylco."

"Have you been her caseworker since she came into care?"

"No," Dawn answered, "I was transferred to this case when the original worker left the agency."

"How long ago was that?"

"Um," she thought about it for a moment before concluding, "around seven months ago."

Sam nodded, "So, if my math is correct, then it was right before the staffing?"

"That's right."

"Did you have an opportunity to visit the Williams-Rice home prior to the staffing?"

"I did," she confirmed. "I met the entire family and toured their house the week before."

"How long was that visit?"

"We probably talked for about thirty minutes," she told him after contemplating it for several seconds.

He nodded, jotting down a few notes before continuing, "What are your thoughts on the Williams-Rice family? Are you supportive of them being Jade's adoptive placement?"

"I am," she said with an enthusiastic nod. "They seem like really good people."

"Yet," he pointed out cautiously, not wanting to come across as confrontational, "the result of the staffing, which you attended, was unanimous support for the Nelsons."

When Dawn didn't answer, only stared at him blankly, he prodded, "Which means you must not have felt that way then?"

Sam studied the woman in front of him. She seemed to be vacillating, indecisive about how to answer. The atmosphere of the room had changed perceptibly with his last couple of questions. He could tell Dawn was nervous. His objective hadn't been to embarrass her, only to prepare for the inevitable questions that would come if she were to testify.

Attempting to reassure her, he said gently, "I'm not trying to put you on the spot, only get us both ready for the things that will certainly be asked if you are called to testify."

"Sure, I get that," she said quickly.

"So are you able to tell me why the support you just voiced for the Williams-Rice family is different than how you voted six-and-a-half months ago?" Sam repeated.

Shrugging, Dawn attempted an explanation, "I guess, you know, I know them better now than I did back then."

Trying to get something more concrete from the caseworker, Sam asked, "Are you saying you would vote differently if the staffing were held today?"

Hesitating again, Dawn mumbled, "I would—I mean, I would

have to consider all the other families also in the staffing, then make a decision on the best one based on that."

It wasn't the answer Sam had hoped for. He attempted another route, "Do you believe Jade has a strong bond with her current foster family?"

"I do," Dawn answered slowly.

"You just wouldn't go so far as to say the original staffing was in error?"

"I don't—" Dawn looked down at her hands, unsure what the best answer was or what the other attendees were saying. She certainly didn't want to get to court and find herself at odds with everyone else who had participated in the staffing. "I don't know."

Sam nodded grimly. His personal belief about the staffing process in this case and more than a few others was that it resulted in a mob mentality. When he had asked Mandi the reasons she thought Dawn seemed so supportive of them at present, yet had also voted against them originally, Mandi told him her impression was that it had more to do with peer pressure instigated by a few rather than sincere conviction one way or the other by each individual involved.

Her analysis matched his own experiences with the process. He knew, however, that Dawn valued her job and her relationship with those peers too much to jeopardize either by shining a spotlight on that. She was a sheep, though she likely had yet to even realize her own role in the situation. Either way, Sam knew Dawn wasn't going to make a very strong witness for Justin or Mandi, if only because she seemed to lack the self-confidence necessary to stand up for what he believed she knew to be in the best interests of the little girl in question.

It's a shame since she's probably spent more time with Jade than anyone else from the Division.

He moved her name to the bottom of the witness list.

"Will you please state your name and your role in the case involving Baby Girl Reylco," Sam requested, starting the recording device.

"Cheri Wilson," the middle-aged woman replied. "I am the manager for Anderson County Child Protective Services, downtown division."

"How did you meet my clients, Mandi Williams and Justin Rice?"

"They were introduced to me after filing a grievance following the staffing for Baby Girl." Cheri answered, adding, "They call her Jade."

"Yes, you're right, thank you." Sam smiled graciously as he continued, "So, you had never heard of my clients, even in their capacity as foster parents, prior to the requested grievance meeting?

"I had not," she confirmed, "but that's typically good. As you can imagine, the things that reach my level are more often related to what's going wrong rather than what's going right. I prefer to believe that most of the time we handle the trust the citizens place in us correctly and, in those instances, my involvement is minimal."

Sam nodded. Although he and Cheri had often been at odds in the past, he sincerely liked the woman, believing her to be motivated by a sincere desire to do the best she could for the children in their care, even if he hadn't always agreed with her conclusions about what that meant. It wasn't hard to imagine how she had risen so far during her tenure with the Division. The majority of her peers simply did not share her tenacity or dedication.

"Do you feel things went wrong with Jade's case?" Sam asked.

Cheri smiled patiently, maternally, at the man a good decade or two ahead of her in life. "I obviously do, given the results of the grievance meeting. Although the staffing was in error, everyone at my level and above has been steadfast in our support of the Williams-Rice family since overturning the original decision."

"What is it that made you certain my clients should be Jade's adoptive resource?"

She responded, "In the course of our discussion, I simply became certain this child already had a home, Mr. Kendal. That's really the sum of it.

"As an agency, we strive to keep children with the families they know, even those that at first glance appear highly dysfunctional. We offer services in an attempt to assist parents who need guidance on how to provide better environments for their children. Sadly, in many cases, they were never shown a better way. We strive to show them.

"In other words, contrary to what many seem to believe — particularly those families that do ultimately lose their kids due to issues they refuse to correct — we are in the business of making families stronger, not tearing them apart. We spend a great deal of money — as an agency, as taxpayers — in an effort to aid the families who wind up on our radar. We remove a child from a home as an absolute last resort. Do you know why that is?"

"I can imagine some reasons," Sam responded, "but I would like to hear the ones you have, as this is your interview."

"The most obvious one is that removing a child from their home is, in the short term at least, often as traumatic as whatever abuse or neglect we are attempting to stop. These children, especially the younger ones, identify with, love and are often fiercely loyal to their families."

She paused to reflect for a moment before sharing, "I remember visiting an eight-year-old girl in the hospital early in my career. Her leg was broken. She had admitted to the nurses that her father had pushed her down the stairs in a fit of rage. It was very obvious how scared she was of the man.

"Yet once she realized he was in a lot of trouble, that she was being taken away, she spent almost an hour explaining to me how bad his day at work had been, how much he needed her and loved her, how she shouldn't have said anything, that she didn't want us to be mad at him, that she didn't want to live anywhere else. She was so desperate to save her father," Cheri grimaced at the memory, "that she couldn't see how desperately she needed to get away from him. I will never forget those big, green eyes imploring me to see things her way."

"But you couldn't, of course," Sam commented empathetically.

"No, we had to take her away," Cheri confirmed, "and ultimately—that woman is grown now—she thanked us for it, but it's always stayed with me: in order to justify putting a child through the trauma of losing their family we better have a damn good reason."

"Sure," Sam agreed.

"So, to put it frankly, in regards to this case, it didn't take long sitting across from the Williams-Rice couple, backed up by all the research I did before and following our conversation with them, to realize we didn't have it in this instance. Maybe they aren't Jade's biological family, but they are the only family she has ever known. And we were about to take her away for what appeared to be nothing more than a number of communication failures before and during the staffing.

"In other words, to answer your original question, what we became certain of in regard to this family is that Jade is thriving in their care, that they are more than capable of providing for her now and in the future, and that there is simply no justification for risking any of that."

With a nod, Sam brought up, "The request the Guardian ad Litem is planning to make at the hearing is not that the Williams-Rices' have their adoption petition denied, but that a second staffing occur. What are your thoughts on that?"

"Unless the commissioner finds the Williams-Rice family unfit, leaving no other interested family," Cheri answered, disappointed to hear it was even being suggested, "I can't imagine him ordering such a thing."

Nodding again, making a note on the paper in front of him, he said, "There are people—more earlier than now, but we should cover it anyway—, who have stated that a child as young as Jade won't be aware of any change in her placement. That the attachment the Williams-Rice family has to her doesn't match her attachment to them. They don't believe it will impact her to be moved."

Cheri shook her head in dismay. "There is so much we don't know about the human mind and its development," she told him, "but there is also an awful lot we do know. More now than ever before in fact. Like that within four months of birth, a baby recognizes its family. We know that within six months they react differently—typically positively—to their parents and siblings. By nine months, they are identifying them with distinct sounds."

"Jade is fourteen-and-a-half-months old," Sam mentioned.

"Right, which puts her well beyond all of those milestones," Cheri nodded, "and, in my entirely non-scientific opinion, that means there is attachment and that it was there even before the staffing. She may not yet be able to articulate all they mean, but to completely uproot her from everything she knows and presume there will be zero psychological impact? That seems a bit of a stretch and, as I mentioned previously, a risk not worth taking when we're talking about a healthy, loving environment."

"I think that covers everything I am going to need," Sam concluded sincerely. "Thank you, Cheri. I am glad we finally have the opportunity to work together on a case."

"It's no problem," she assured him, though certainly they both had ample evidence to the contrary.

"I believe you will be a strong witness for my clients. You have been an invaluable advocate so far."

"It is our honor and privilege to work with children and families," Cheri said, with another kind smile. "We appreciate the grace with which this family has handled such a trying situation."

Sam nodded his agreement.

Cheri continued, "Our sole interest at this point is making certain Jade's current home life continues without interruption. I am more than happy to do my part in the hopes of achieving that end."

"If you don't mind, please begin by telling me your name and your role with the Division," Sam prompted for the third time that day.

"Natalie Mills," the oversized woman replied, "adoption specialist with Anderson County Children's Protective Services Division."

Sam nodded, "Thank you. Will you please share with me your role in the adoption process?"

"You've worked with the Division enough that I would think you should know by now," Natalie joked.

Smiling patiently, Sam reminded her, "This is just a matter of due course, Ms. Mills. I want to make certain I properly grasp everything."

"Sure, of course," she acknowledged, answering, "I am the one who sends out notices that a child is available for adoption. I receive the home studies of families interested in adopting the child, then narrow those down to a group of four or five couples or families. Once that's done, I set up the staffing to include all relevant individuals.

"Once the staffing has occurred, I put together all the information we have on the child and send it to the selected family. Once they accept the information sent to them and confirm they still wish to proceed, I complete all the paperwork and submit it to the mandated parties, including the Division's attorney, the Guardian ad Litem and the court."

"Do you recall the staffing for Baby Girl Reylco?"

"It would be unbelievable if I didn't," Natalie laughed sarcastically. "After all, that's what everyone is so up-in-arms about."

Taken aback by her tone, Sam asked, "Is that the atmosphere at the Division?"

"No," Natalie corrected herself. "I just mean that's what all this commotion is related to, isn't it? No one has had a chance to forget about it is all I'm saying."

The woman in front of Sam was obviously exasperated, but he decided not to pursue the issue. Instead, he moved on to the next question, "What were your impressions of the staffing?"

"The contents of a staffing are considered confidential," Natalie informed him rigidly, "unless I am called to testify."

"That's correct," Sam agreed, "however I am not asking you to convey individual sentiments made at the staffing or replay it in its entirety — all definitely confidential matters — but I would like to know your personal impressions of it."

"At the time it seemed like any other staffing," she replied with a begrudging shrug.

Sam nodded encouragingly.

"Until, you know," Natalie continued, a bit of an edge creeping into her voice again, "your clients decided to throw a temper tantrum because it didn't turn out the way they wanted."

Letting the remark go, Sam went instead for the heart of the issue, "Then you don't support Mandi and Justin as the adoptive resource for Jade?"

"I didn't say that," Natalie responded impatiently. "All I know is that Baby Girl's case was going along without any issues until they filed that grievance."

Sam nodded again.

"They have caused me quite a bit of extra work," Natalie pointed out in defensive response to his silence. "Do you know I had to redo every piece of paperwork I had already prepared for the Nelsons?"

"I'm sure." Sam agreed, manufacturing a sympathetic tone, though unable to resist adding, "Mandi and Justin have felt a degree of inconvenience as well. Yet their stance seems to be that it is worth some degree of discomfort in order to make certain this child ends up with the correct family. I know, being this is your field of specific interest, that you feel the same."

He hadn't asked it as a question, but Natalie felt the need to respond with a tight-lipped, "Of course."

Sam didn't believe there was any need to pursue questioning Natalie much further. He could tell she was too resentful about her workload to have any specific concern for Jade or the tenuous situation the Williams-Rice family found themselves in.

She likely won't cause us any problems, if only because another family being selected will generate even more work, but neither will she be of much assistance, Sam thought grimly.

"Your name and role with the Division, please."

"Jean Pamela. I have been with the agency close to forty years," the woman in her mid-sixties answered.

Sam was unable to disguise his surprise, remarking, "With such a high turnover rate at the Division, you obviously have more tenacity than most."

"Maybe," Jean laughed good-naturedly, "but I truly enjoy working with the families who come into our care. It's not a perfect system, but I believe in what we do. I am currently a licensing manager. I have been working in that role for the past seven years."

"Specifically, you are the licensing manager for Justin Rice and Mandi Williams?"

Jean nodded in confirmation, saying, "That's correct."

"What are your responsibilities as a licensing manager?"

"I am the one who meets with prospective foster and adoptive families to make sure they, their home, and their lifestyle are to the standards set forth by the state. I do this during the application process, as well as at regular intervals throughout the remainder of time the family is in service."

Curiosity piqued, Sam asked, "What do you mean by lifestyle?"

"You know," Jean laughed easily, "no drugs, no criminal convictions, and no excessive beliefs in one direction or another. Things like that."

"Marriage?"

As the manager for Mandi and Justin, Jean was aware their lack of a marriage license was the issue suspected to be at the root of their not being selected as Jade's adoptive resource. She answered Sam's question thoughtfully, "In accordance with the law, we don't specifically require a marriage license. My role is to judge the suitability of a couple or family to assist the children in the state's care. The state does not require partners to be married in order to be foster or adoptive families. What it does require is that we investigate the nature of all adult relationships within a household to determine if those are appropriate and healthy for children to be subjected to."

"How do you do that?"

"Well," Jean explained, "we start with the basics, just sitting down and talking to them. We are looking for things like commitment to the home and the family, stability, a long term plan for the children."

"As Mandi and Justin were permitted to become a foster family and potential adoptive resource," Sam said, "you must have decided they met the criteria?"

"Without question," Jean answered. "To be quite honest, we were and are very impressed by what this young family has and is accomplishing."

"So the lack of marriage wasn't an issue for you?"

"Absolutely not," she responded. "This is not a couple who met at a bar the weekend before showing up to become foster parents. They had a child to whom they were quite obviously devoted, they felt a need to give something back for all the support Mandi received during the loss of her mother as a teenager, and they have the resources and community to support their lifestyle and goals. I have met married couples I wouldn't put as much faith in as I do in those two."

Sam was pleased by the unequivocal support being voiced for his clients. "That's quite a ringing endorsement," he commented.

"It is the truth," Jean shrugged. "I have spent a significant amount of time with this family and I've worked with quite a few families during my time with CPS. I have no doubts about them or I wouldn't hesitate to say so."

"I believe it," Sam smiled, then asked seriously, "Your impressions match my own experiences with my clients. They seem to have it together."

"Yes, they do."

"Having said that, what is your opinion on what went wrong at the staffing for Baby Girl?"

After thinking about it a moment, Jean said slowly, "I feel as if—of course I couldn't avoid it and who knows if it would have really made a difference—but this... this entire situation shouldn't have happened. I felt bad the other family got dragged into it—"

"The Nelsons," Sam acknowledged with a nod.

"—but that staffing never should have gone the way it did. Who's to say if my being there would have changed anything, but..." Her voice trailed off as she shrugged again.

Not wanting to say the wrong thing or appear to be leading her, Sam spoke carefully, "My clients and I have discussed your absence from that particular meeting. They shared their feelings that a number of things went wrong that morning and then snowballed so to speak... Your inability to attend was definitely mentioned as one of those things. They feel Lauren was well-intentioned but simply wasn't able to speak in their defense and, having never been to a staffing themselves, they weren't prepared to pick up the slack."

"Right," Jean agreed regretfully. "Truth be told, they didn't even know to expect questions. We always tell the foster parents not to plan on articulating their interest in adopting the child because their licensing manager will speak to that once they have updated the group on the child's progress and left. Otherwise, it could give them an unfair advantage. They are just to show up in the capacity of foster parents updating on a child in their care."

"Understood," Sam replied, jotting down a few notes. Looking back up at Jean, he asked, "Now, are you going to be able to make it to the hearing?"

"I have a few more doctors appointments," Jean told him, "but the hearing date is on my calendar, so I definitely intend to be there.

"I don't want anyone testifying for me," she added. "I don't think it ever should have been suggested Jade be moved and I especially don't believe that now. And I have no problem getting up on the stand to say as much!"

Sam nodded with satisfaction. Between Jean and Cheri, he had two very strong witnesses for the Williams-Rice family to counter whatever witness Payton planned to call. Mandi had been right to insist he speak with both.

"You know, their foster care license is set to expire in a few months," Jean remarked as they were wrapping things up.

"Is it?" Sam asked with polite curiosity, unaware of that fact or why she was bringing it up.

Jean nodded, "I think we're going to lose them."

"They have been put through quite a bit this year," Sam responded carefully, not wanting to offend Jean or put words in his clients' mouths. "I haven't discussed it with them though, so I have no idea their intentions."

"I understand," she acknowledged with a grimace. "It's just one of the biggest frustrations I have, how this agency burns the good families out, often leaving behind only those taking in kids for the absolute wrong reasons."

17 – Day 482

Mandi had received the email from Natalie yesterday afternoon. Although she was typically very prompt about answering electronic correspondence given that her job kept her almost continually connected, she found herself delaying. Natalie's questions were simple, yet her attempts to answer them kept getting muddled by the aggravation of the larger situation.

> I am working on a report for court later this month. Are there any updates? Eating/Sleeping well? What is she eating? Teeth?
>
> Natalie Mills
> Adoption Worker, Anderson County

Re-reading the email, Mandi grimaced. She didn't want to be painted as anything less than helpful, but it was not lost on her that Natalie had often been exactly that.

She noted the lack of proper, professional greeting or introduction.

She noted that Natalie apparently wondered if their daughter was eating teeth.

She noted the lack of thank you, sincerely, or any other form of polite closure.

Baby Girl

She noted the subject—Baby Girl—and was reminded of Natalie's outright refusal to call the 16-month-old by anything except her legal, completely generic name.

"Natalie's not going to make a great advocate for our position...," is one of the statements Sam had made several weeks earlier when reporting on how the witness interviews had gone. Mandi had not been surprised by the information. It was clear from Natalie's demeanor how personally she took the fact *her* staffing had ultimately been overturned.

Natalie is just another example of the unprofessional attitudes and opinions in our way. Attitudes and opinions which have little to do with Jade or the very good life she is having.

Natalie, as with all of their objectors, didn't have a specific complaint about Jade's care now or in the past, yet that didn't prevent her—anymore than any of the others—from continuing to construct hurdles just, it seemed, for the sake of constructing them.

Everyone is terribly inconvenienced by our stance and they want to make certain we know it. I suppose they think, unlike them, we're thoroughly enjoying the upheaval to our lives.

Mandi quickly typed out a response, her aggravation at the forefront.

Hey Natalie,

I was just wondering if you might be able to tell me why Child Protective Services hires such piss ignorant people and then put the lives of small, helpless children at their mercy?

I did some math today. Jade has been alive approximately 11,568 hours. She has been in the care of this state for almost as long. Jade joined us when she was fifteen days, or approximately 360 hours, old. That gives us 11,208 hours of bonding and getting to know and nurture "baby girl." All numbers are approximate, of course, except for this one: three. That's the number of hours you have spent with her or us. Three. Out of 11,208.

Listen, I get that you are all overworked and underpaid. I am not suggesting you ever had more than three hours to spare for this child. I don't believe you were goofing off or in any other way being intentionally neglectful of your duties. You have too many kids and too little time. I get that.

But the facts are the facts. And the biggest fact of all, which you and a handful of others seem hell-bent on ignoring, is that Jade is obviously happy and thriving in our care; which means we can't be the terrible people you are hoping. So I'm just wondering, does the small box your thoughts are confined to come with a key?

The name she answers to is Jade.

Learn to start and end an email properly. Professional courtesy is never inappropriate.

Take the time to get to know the kids in your care or just admit you don't know and stay out of the way.

That's all.

Sincerely,
Mandi

In reality, of course, it wasn't an email Mandi could seriously send. She realized, as well, that the response was more than a little out of proportion with Natalie's inquiry. The hostility was related more to the cumulative effect of all the little things they had tolerated from people like her for months now.

Mandi and Justin had lived and been raised in such a way — striving to be prolific, thoughtful members of society — that they were unaccustomed to being at the mercy of other's stupidity. The simple-minded, poisonous individuals they were suffering at this point were not the kind of people they would have ever allowed to linger in their or their children's lives prior to this experience. To not only have them in their lives but to be at their mercy...

It was the worst kind of torture. The only thing that kept Justin and her from telling them off was the knowledge those actions wouldn't ultimately be beneficial to their goal of adopting Jade.

It's getting harder and harder to exercise restraint, Mandi thought grimly, backspacing through the initial draft of her email.

"I can't believe how big she's gotten!" Dawn exclaimed from where she was sitting on the couch in the living room.

Mandi and Jade were going into work and daycare late so Dawn could complete her last home visit before the adoption hearing.

"It is unbelievable," Mandi agreed from where she was sitting on the floor, next to Jade. They were surrounded by plastic food from the toddler's play kitchen. "I was looking at some pictures of her from those first days she spent here and it is stunning how much she has changed."

"You know, I was actually one of the emergency workers on call when she came into care. Another worker and I went to pick her up from the hospital."

Surprised, Mandi said, "You were? I never knew that. I didn't think you met her until you took over for Racquel."

Dawn nodded, "Well, we didn't stay very long. We weren't aware they wouldn't let us be the ones to pick her up, so we pretty much showed up and met her only to be told hospital policy wouldn't allow her to be discharged to us."

"That's right," Mandi remembered with a nod. "They wanted the family she would be staying with to pick her up. They have a NICU policy requiring the caretaker prove they know how to feed the child. Racquel made such a big deal about making certain we could pick her for that reason that we thought she had serious health issues!"

Dawn laughed at the memory, "That's because she actually had a foster family before you all lined up to take Jade—"

"Really?" Mandi raised her eyebrows in surprise.

"—but when the mother heard she had to pick Baby Girl up from the hospital herself, she refused. Said she wasn't going to no hospital 'cause she already knew how to feed a baby."

"Wow. Huh," Mandi responded thoughtfully, looking over at the girl toddling around with a plastic red pepper sticking out of her mouth.

"Did the kids go down okay?" Mandi asked Justin over the phone. She was working late to make up for the time she had missed due to the home visit with Dawn earlier in the day. "How are you feeling about everything?"

"The kids went down without any problems. Little Jade was very tired." Addressing her second question, he told her, "I am feeling angry and pissed. I feel as if someone is threatening to take our kid away and, honestly, I want to just beat the crap out of them!"

"I know what you mean," Mandi grimaced, "Did something specific happen or are you just thinking about the days ahead? It's hard to keep being nice. Trust me, I know. That's the main reason I hope they find in our favor Thursday instead of continuing to prolong things... I'm really not sure how much longer I can hold my tongue."

"That's what I'm pissed about. I want to run and scream about how asinine all this is! I'm angry about the angst and money we've had to pour into this when we never did anything wrong."

"As long as we get to keep Jade, I know we can bounce back from the rest," Mandi reassured him. "We just need Commissioner Roberts to see what everyone supporting us sees. Sooner rather than later."

"That's the truth," he agreed, "and I know we can bounce back. I am just worried about losing Jade. If Roberts says no, then what on earth is so bad about us? They give some pretty terrible parents every chance in the world to keep their kids and don't give us one?"

"We don't know that yet," Mandi corrected him, looking at her dry erase board, at all the things that still needed to be completed for the project she was working on. "He might. He should. There is no good reason why he won't. I am more worried about it getting sent back to a staffing because I feel as if that's where the politics come into play. I hope Kendal is ready for that. He said his argument is going to be that it doesn't make sense because the Nelsons could have stayed in and we aren't going away even if the second staffing doesn't select us."

"Heck no, we aren't," Justin agreed resolutely.

"I just don't want this to drag on any longer. The uncertainty is unbearable. If we haven't proven our love and dedication to Jade is the equivalent of a biological child by now, then I can't honestly guess what else we can do."

"Yeah, this is out of hand," he sighed. "Jade is very much worth it. I'm just tired of playing the game."

"I know. I am too."

"I'll be good and happy for court. I'm just pissed off tonight. I'm really feeling the pressure this week, can't seem to get it off my mind."

"Trust me," Mandi assured him, thinking of her reaction to Natalie's email. "I understand. It's a roller coaster right now."

When Mandi got home later that night, everyone was in bed. She sat down at her computer, reflecting on the events of the day. Specifically, on the story Dawn had told her about the first foster family selected for Jade; about how if the foster mother had been willing to show up at the hospital, each of their lives would be drastically different right now.

We would have missed the miracle of Jade completely.

It was humbling to think just how many little things fell perfectly into place at just the right time to result in their daughter's life with them. One thing, one decision, in any different direction and none of it would have happened.

We would have missed out on so much.

In that moment, it occurred to Mandi there was perhaps a more productive letter she could write than her earlier email to Natalie; one that might better help get her in the right frame of mind for the hearing looming a little over a week away.

She started to type:

Dear Mr. Reylco,

You don't know me, yet we are bound to each other through events neither of us could have predicted seventeen months ago. I am the mother of the foster family your daughter came to live with after she was discharged from the hospital. We call her Jade, though legally her name is still Baby Girl.

Despite what have obviously been difficult decisions and circumstances in your life—and I'm not here to judge—I want to believe the best about you. As a foster family, we have seen so many parents try to keep their children, often to their children's detriment, when they shouldn't. You didn't do that and I respect the very difficult decision you made. I want to believe you leaving

Baby Girl

Jade at the police station in the days after she was born was an act of love based on clarity, knowing that it was the best you could offer the little girl you helped bring into this world.

My belief in that, accurate or not, is why I write to you now.

Next week we are headed to court. The purpose is two-fold. First, we are going to request the termination of your rights as her father. Your absence this past seventeen months makes this being granted almost a certainty. Second, we want to make official Jade's place in our family—to adopt the little girl you left in the state's care.

I will be honest with you. The second task has proven much more difficult than the first. Even now, less than a week from the hearing, we have no guarantee the commissioner will side with us. We must simply wait to find out what his decision will be.

Waiting is very difficult, Mr. Reylco. We have been waiting for months. Jade has not waited. She has grown in physical, mental and emotional ability. She is unbelievably happy. She is fearless when it comes to trying new things and exploring the world around her. She has reached many milestones. She babbles, she runs, she is quick to smile. She loves water slides and discovering new things.

She has a family. Not just a mom and a dad, but a brother and grandparents and cousins and aunts and uncles. Important for you to know is that this family does not take anything away from her biological family. We are aware she has a half-sibling and we are supportive of them meeting if the day ever comes. We are aware she has an older grandmother that it might be good for her to meet before too many years pass. We are also aware her path is likely to one day include you in some form or another. We are okay with that.

We want Jade to always feel complete and loved and accepted both by making her 100% a member of our family and by respecting the entirety of her story and, by extension, yours. In short, we want to give her whatever she might need now and in the future. We believe ourselves to be capable of that.

We have fought hard for Jade this past year; harder as the months went on. Our devotion to her has only grown with each day. If your intention in giving her up was the hope she would find a fiercely protective, loving and loyal family... I want you to know that—no matter what happens next week—we have done everything in our power to provide that. Our conviction is that she is in a home better than what you could have ever hoped.

We are so very grateful for the brave decision you made that led her to us. We have not taken—nor will we ever take—lightly the life that has forever changed ours.

Sincerely,

Mandi Williams

18 – Day 491

Commissioner Roberts was already seated when they filed in, which was typical procedure for family court. It didn't make sense for him to exit and re-enter the room between every case on the docket, as some were completed in as little as a few minutes. The courtroom was called to order when the commissioner indicated to the bailiff he was ready to begin.

Waiting for everyone to take their seats, Mandi studied the man out of the corner of her eye. He was probably in his mid-forties, severe looking, but had always seemed intent on getting the details straight by paying careful attention to the matters placed before him. Mandi hoped he would be able to cut through all the white noise of their situation in order to get to the relevant facts buried underneath.

Specifically, that we are the best family for Jade. The only family.

Shortly after ten, the Commissioner said, "Counselors, are we ready to begin?"

All eyes turned toward the middle of the courtroom where the attorneys sat. Due to the fact family court often involved multiple parties represented by various legal counsel, the classic plaintiff and defense tables were absent in favor of a single, long table perpendicular to the commissioner's bench.

After everyone had nodded, he continued, "Very well. Please introduce yourselves for the purposes of court record."

As the individuals at the table began to introduce themselves, Mandi looked around. She and Justin were seated at the table, directly across from their attorney. The three of them were closest to the commissioner. To Mandi's right was Natalie. Across from her, to Sam's left, was the attorney for the Division. Based on what Sam had conveyed to them, Mandi didn't expect to hear much from him, as he had no dog in this fight given CPS was now supporting their petition. To the attorney's left sat Dawn. At the end of the table, furthest from the commissioner, was Payton.

A single row of chairs lined the back wall. Each one of them was occupied, as Sam had made good on his plan to make certain each of their supporters was at the hearing. In a quick glance, Mandi recognized Jean Pamela, Lauren Sampson, Cheri Wilson, Valerie Francis, Kelsey Carson, Deanna Randolph, Dr. Castle, as well as a handful of friends and family who had insisted on being present.

Mandi felt overwhelmed by the incredible show of support. Some of these people were hired, but many of them simply believed in the role Mandi and Justin were playing in Jade's life. Since the day they had started their fight, not only had their immediate friends and family rallied around them, but those individuals' friends and families—having heard about and been moved by their story—also wrapped their arms around them. From the mother of Mandi's friend who made Jade her own adoption quilt to the co-worker of Justin's who put their family on the church prayer list and everyone in between... they had been met at every twist, every speed bump, by the unwavering support of their community.

This is what they mean by it taking the entire village, Mandi thought

Baby Girl

with gratitude. *We may have felt lonely at times, lost in our struggle, but alone is fortunately something we have never truly been.*

Introductions complete, Commissioner Roberts said, "Mr. Kendal, your motion for the court to grant the adoption of Baby Girl to Mandi Williams and Justin Rice is before us this morning. Please proceed."

"Thank you, your honor," Sam started. "As you mentioned, we are here this morning in the interest of Baby Girl Reylco, whom my clients refer to as Jade. We have before the court a motion requesting that the adoption of Baby Girl be granted on this day, the child having resided with the Williams-Rice family for the past sixteen-and-a-half month, since she was just fifteen-days-old."

The commissioner nodded.

"Your honor, as Guardian ad Litem for the child," Payton spoke up briskly, "we are against the adoption petition being granted at this time, as we do not feel it is ultimately in the best interest of the child to remain with this family permanently."

"You have not asked that Jade—er—Baby Girl be moved from this foster home in the sixteen-plus months she has been there," Commissioner Roberts noted, "yet you are still objecting to the appointment of Ms. Williams and Mr. Rice as her adoptive parents. It seems we have been here before. What is the reason for your position?"

Standing up to address the inquiry, Payton replied, "We are simply asking that a new staffing take place. Our objection is to the fact a decision that took half a day and twelve people to make was turned over by two people after a one hour meeting with Ms. Williams and Mr. Rice. There is a procedure in place for a reason and we believe it should be utilized. I don't believe we want to set a precedent for circumnavigating the staffing process."

"My understanding," Kendal countered evenly, "is that my clients knew the outcome of the staffing by 10:30, which means it didn't last any longer than *maybe* two hours. In addition to that, they were only in attendance for about twenty minutes of the meeting, which makes the hour Valerie and Cheri spent with them one-on-one quite lengthy in comparison.

"Irrespective of those points, it seems relevant to point out, your honor," he looked from Payton to the commissioner, "that the grievance process is in fact a part of and a valid response to any undertaking by the Division, including a staffing."

He turned back to the Guardian ad Litem, "Unless you are suggesting that a meeting of fallible humans can somehow produce an infallible result every time and, therefore, the grievance process should be done away with entirely?"

Mandi could all but see the steam pouring out of Payton's ears. It wasn't as gratifying as one would expect. She and Justin would have preferred if the woman had merely taken the time to get to know them instead of playing politics with their daughter. Her inability to do that left everything hinging on the decision of one man, a disconcerting proposition at best.

"Obviously I'm not," Payton snapped. "As I have stated previously, our belief is that if the first staffing found a more suitable placement, then a second staffing will as well."

"In regards to that," Sam responded squarely, "perhaps you can explain what is suitable or consistent about the selection of a family on state aide, no children, in poor health, with reports indicating suspicion of fundamentalist religious inclinations?"

"What are we talking about, counsel?" Roberts asked Kendal irately.

Mandi involuntarily tensed at the ire directed at their attorney.

"I apologize, your honor," Sam turned back toward the bench. He clarified, "The Nelsons are the family the first staffing chose for this little girl, the one the Guardian ad Litem's office is so up in arms about. A family that couldn't be more opposite from my clients."

Payton didn't say anything.

"You likely don't remember them because they never made it to court," Sam went on, "as they requested their petition be dismissed in exchange for monetary compensation from the Division, so deep was their interest and love for this little girl."

"They didn't have much choice but to back off once your clients refused to honor the decision made at the staffing," Payton shot back.

"Oh, they had choices," Sam corrected her. "The reality is, we showed them the findings from the staffing along with the reasons it was overturned and I believe they drew the only conclusion they could, which is that the staffing itself was a gross misunderstanding or miscalculation. There is no reason, Commissioner, to presume it will be any better the second time around or that my clients will simply disappear if another one is requested or another resource selected."

"Alright, counselors," Roberts said with a sigh, "I can tell this is going to be a process. If we can get back to my original question, though," he looked at Payton. "You say your office is only seeking another staffing, but there must be some reason you object to the petitioners, regardless of how they got here, or surely you wouldn't be recommending the state expend the amount of time and money a second staffing will require."

"We believe there are issues with the petitioners," Payton said vaguely. "Issues that were present at the staffing, which might be able to be overlooked while they are only a temporary placement for Baby

Girl, but not under consideration as a long-term placement."

"She has been with my clients for well over a year," Sam pointed out. "I am not certain *temporary* is a word that applies to that length of time."

Payton scowled.

"Alright," Roberts said again, holding up his hands. He looked at Payton, "Since I'm obviously not going to get a clear answer, let's just get started. Ms. Gringo, to be clear, your motion is not necessarily that the Williams-Rice adoption petition be rejected, but that another staffing be ordered to see if a more suitable family can be found?"

"That's correct, your honor," she confirmed with a nod.

Turning to Sam, he continued, "Mr. Kendal, your desire is that the adoption petition from your clients be heard and decided on today?"

"Yes, your honor," Sam answered. "This little girl has been waiting a long while for the court to recognize as hers the family she is already with. There are no grounds for continuing to waste more time and resources on what is already a healthy, loving placement."

"Fine," Roberts remarked, making some notes. "Ms. Gringo, call your first witness."

"I don't have any witnesses to call," Payton informed him, shifting uneasily in her seat. "I believe our position is clear."

"That's an interesting approach, Ms. Gringo," Commissioner Roberts remarked dryly. He turned to Sam, "Do you have witnesses or am I to decide this case based solely on each of your respective opinions?"

Payton blushed, angry at Leslie for refusing to testify at the last minute, even angrier at Edith for putting her in this situation. She hadn't subpoenaed the woman because her presence had been guaranteed by Edith. Payton knew she looked like fool and she resented it.

"We have a list of witnesses we can call," Sam answered, referring to the full row of seats across the back of the room, "but if Ms. Gringo has no witnesses, I will only need to interview Ms. Williams and Mr. Rice."

"Please proceed," the commissioner directed. "We'll let Ms. Gringo start with any questions she might have for your clients, then allow you finish with each."

Sam nodded, "That sounds fine."

"Has it ever been too much, dealing with the process of this adoption?" Payton asked.

"It was always too much," Justin answered honestly. "Always," he continued with a slight shrug, "but we just tried not to think about it. That wasn't always easy, and it didn't always work, but that's what we tried to do. We strived to just focus on the moment... on the fact we had both of our children with us at least for the time being."

Mandi felt her eyes burn.

All the months of uncertainty, these final hours, minutes, of uncertainty...

"Do you have any regrets?"

Justin cleared his throat nervously, "Only that I didn't realize the moment we got the phone call about Jade how much I wanted that little girl in our lives."

Confused, Payton asked, "What do you mean?"

"When Mandi first told me she was going to pick up this baby with potential health problems, I—I didn't think it was a good idea." He confessed, "I didn't want her to do it."

"Hmm," Payton nodded, more than willing to let Justin dig

himself into a hole.

"Don't get me wrong," Justin clarified quickly, sensing the disapproval at his words, "it wasn't even an hour or two after meeting Jade that I was totally on board—heck, it probably wasn't even ten minutes—, but... but when all this slid out of control so many months ago, I admit part of me wondered if it wasn't somehow punishment for my early reservations."

Mandi shook her head sadly. She could see his eyes were red, knew he was holding back tears. He had expressed this fear—that they were somehow being punished for his initial hesitation—more than once since the staffing. It had surprised her, as Justin had never been one to prescribe grand, overlying schemes to the random events of life.

I wish he wouldn't be so hard on himself.

There was a lot Mandi didn't know when she insisted on picking up Jade that afternoon. In fact, immediately following that first call, most reasonable people likely would have sided with Justin. Once Mandi made up her mind something was right, though, it took a lot to convince her differently. It only meant their approaches were different, not that her heart had been any more sincere or true than his.

She had also certainly had her share of questions and doubts on the road to this day. What she had ultimately realized, however, is that merely having those thoughts, those queries, didn't make a particular conclusion inevitable. It simply meant the mind was doing what the mind does: assessing a situation with the desire to find the most sensible path forward. It didn't mean it knew what that path was, that it could guess beyond the incomplete information it possessed in the moment or even that it could ultimately overrule what the heart demanded despite practical limitations.

That Justin had ended up grateful he hadn't succeeded in

detouring Mandi—instead falling madly in love with Jade within those first hours—was reason enough why he didn't deserve any retribution. He had been committed to their daughter without reservation from almost the moment he laid eyes on her.

Mandi knew there wasn't a life force in the universe who would begrudge him an hour of doubt when the seventeen months since had been filled with nothing but certainty and love. She hoped when all this was finally behind them, he would be able to recognize that.

"I don't have any further questions for Mr. Rice," Payton concluded.

Commissioner Roberts made some notes as he prompted, "Mr. Kendal? Questions for Mr. Rice?"

"Just a few," Sam replied. He looked at Justin, commenting, "You have been put through quite a bit the past nine months."

Justin nodded, "We have."

"Why not just give up?"

Surprised, Justin stared at their lawyer for a second before answering, a bit incredulously, "She's our daughter. We are all she knows. It got hard, but giving up was never a legitimate option. We wouldn't give up on any of our children."

"But you must have had moments during this process…" Kendal pushed, "Doubts?"

Justin thought of those initial hours after the staffing. He answered carefully, "We were shocked and hurt when we found out we weren't selected originally. There was a period of… reevaluation."

"What were you reevaluating? Your love for Jade? Your dedication to her?"

"Whether or not we were right," Justin said candidly. "We were devastated, but we had to honestly consider whether or not these individuals at the staffing saw something we didn't."

"And?"

"And we knew they didn't; that their perception—however it was arrived at—was wrong. We knew they had walked in with their minds made up before they even took the time to speak with us. We drew strength from our friends and our family, we spoke to attorneys... We learned a little more about the system and the individual players in the staffing that day. We learned of the biases each brought to the table."

"Biases?"

"We came to believe the real issue was a woman from the Guardian ad Litem's office, Edith Scarlett," Justin conveyed matter-of-factly, "who has a history of taking particular offense to non-traditional families, especially when it comes to the adoption of healthy children. She was the one who asked most of the questions at the staffing, the one who barely let us respond, the one who heard of the mysterious hotline no one could ever find record of."

Payton stared down at her papers, her face expressionless.

Sam remarked, "Those biases obviously weren't enough to stop you from moving forward."

"No, we came to understand we were expected to simply yield to their decision... but we got to the point where we knew that wasn't an option."

"Why?"

"Even if we lost our daughter, we wanted to make certain to put a voice to what had gone wrong at that staffing. We may have questioned ourselves in those first hours after we learned the outcome—I think that's probably a normal thing for conscientious, introspective people to do—but once we decided our course, we were all in. Ups and downs. She is our daughter and if they wanted our daughter, they were going to have to fight us for her."

"Have you ever regretted fighting for Jade?"

"No," Justin responded immediately, shaking his head firmly, "No. We would go through all of this and much, *much* more for her or our son, Matthew."

"Ms. Gringo, do you have questions for Ms. Williams?" Commissioner Roberts asked.

"No, your honor, I don't," Payton answered.

Sam looked at the Guardian ad Litem in surprise.

"Mr. Kendal?" Roberts prompted.

"I do, Commissioner, and I'm honestly shocked Ms. Gringo has chosen to demur, given the accusations she and her colleagues have leveled against my clients both today and in the past several months," Sam responded.

Payton rolled her eyes.

"Please just begin, Mr. Kendal," Roberts said in exasperation, rubbing his temples.

Turning to Mandi, he began his cross examination by saying, "The Guardian ad Litem has previously alluded to possible *issues* specific to your past. Are you aware of that?"

"I am," Mandi acknowledged.

"What is your understanding of what those issues are?"

"They seem to be related to the fact my mother was killed in a car accident when I was fifteen and the psychiatrist my father sent me to after that. He briefly put me on anti-anxiety medication. There was also concern expressed about my desire to talk to a therapist after a friend was killed in a car accident six years ago."

"Have you succeeded despite these particular challenges in your life?"

Mandi laughed in spite of herself, "I've done alright."

He waited.

She grew serious, "Yes, I've been in my current career for over thirteen years. I have a beautiful family. I have accomplished many of the personal goals I have set for myself. Life isn't perfect—*I'm* not perfect—, I still have much to learn and I suspect that will continue until the day I die, but it's a good life."

"Ms. Gringo has suggested that perhaps the challenges you have faced make you unfit for the role of parent to this or, we presume, any child—"

Commissioner Roberts brow noticeably furrowed in confusion, though he didn't make eye contact with anyone in particular.

"I never said that—" Payton spoke up angrily, rising from her chair in protest.

"Oh," Kendal replied, appearing perplexed, "I thought when you demanded a psychological evaluation a few months ago…"

"We just wanted to make certain Ms. Williams had addressed those issues which previously existed for her."

"Was the psychological evaluation completed?" Commissioner Roberts interjected, wanting to move the proceedings forward.

Payton sat down, her face red with anger.

"It was, your honor," Sam confirmed.

"What were the results of the evaluation? Do you have them with you?" Roberts questioned.

Reaching into a folder he had sitting on the table, Kendal extracted the letter from Dr. Castle. He handed it to the commissioner, saying, "These results are also on file with the court."

Roberts pursed his lips as he read the letter, then passed it back across the bench to Kendal, asking, "Is Dr. Castle present today?"

"He is, your Honor," Sam confirmed motioning to the man sitting against the back wall.

"The report before me states that you concluded this couple is a suitable adoptive resource," Roberts directed his statement at the psychologist. "Is that the assessment you made?"

"Yes, your Honor," Castle confirmed with a nod. "I found no cause for concern during the individual interview or testing."

Looking at Payton, Roberts inquired, "Have you had the opportunity to review the letter from Dr. Castle?"

Payton acknowledged, "I have."

"Do you have any questions or objections related to it?" Roberts pressed.

"No, your honor," Payton gritted her teeth, "I don't. We feel there are other issues unrelated to Ms. Williams' evaluation, specifically the lack of legitimacy to how the staffing was overturned."

Sam opened his mouth to protest.

"Alright," Commissioner Roberts cut in with a resigned sigh, "we've already covered the staffing and I believe I'm clear on everyone's position related to that. I do have other cases to get to so there's no need to revisit the subject. As to the evaluation, if there are no objections, the court will accept the doctor's findings."

The courtroom was silent for a moment, as the commissioner wrote down some information. Finally, he asked, "Mr. Kendal, do you have further questions for Ms. Williams?"

"Yes, your honor, a couple," Sam responded. Turning to Mandi, he asked, "This has been a terrible experience for you as well, hasn't it?"

Mandi hesitated, admitting, "It's been stressful. We have had to live with the possibility of losing our daughter. A daughter that—

while we have waited for others to decide our fate—we have fallen more in love with as each day passes. It's a tough..." Mandi swallowed past the lump in her throat, "It's a tough reality to live with, the idea that she could be taken away."

"I bet. You have probably lost quite a bit of faith in the system."

"No, I—" Mandi paused. She thought of Cheri, Valerie, even Payton. "No," she started again. "I mean, do we wish it had been easier? Sure. Are there things that need to be looked at and fixed? Definitely. But there was a lot of good along the way. We weren't allowed to fall far before we found the support we needed to continue our fight... Not to mention, even if the system has hurt us, it's also the same one that handed us our daughter to begin with. Those things aren't moot simply because the journey has been more difficult than we expected or feel it should have been."

Kendal turned to the rest of the room, "I remember when I interviewed the Williams-Rices' licensing manager several weeks ago, she expressed her confidence that Mandi could and would always find the bright side to everything; that she had a knack for turning loss into gain. I think you," he looked back at his client, "have proven her right once again."

Mandi could see Jean nodding from her seat along the back row. She felt tears sting her eyes at the unexpected praise. Internally, she squirmed uncomfortably under the weight of the admiring words.

They had walked their path as best they could.

Have we walked it well? Probably.

Have we walked it perfectly? No.

Mandi thought of the hole still in the bedroom wall at home, hidden from view by a strategically placed picture frame. She comforted herself with the knowledge that moments like those had

Baby Girl

been few—with that having truly been the worst—and that their kids had been shielded from the majority of it.

"I have no further questions, your honor," Sam said.

The courtroom had been quiet for several minutes. Commissioner Roberts was looking down at some paperwork on his bench, the contents of which were a mystery to the remainder of the room.

"I was just glancing at this financial statement," he finally said, before another lengthy pause.

The remark puzzled Mandi, who wasn't entirely certain what the commissioner was referring to. She knew their income was one of the few things that had never come into question. In fact, given the dubious suitability of the Nelsons based on that verity alone, the opposing parties had largely avoided any mention of it, even after the Nelsons had requested their petition be dismissed.

"Do you have any supporting documentation for the extent of these legal fees?" Commissioner Roberts asked, disbelief etched on his face as he looked up at Kendal, "Is this number really accurate?"

Rising from his seat, Kendal approached the bench. At that moment, Mandi could see the document under review was one that stated the total cost they had paid to date in their struggle for Jade.

"Yes, your honor, that's correct," Sam confirmed, "and we do have files of documentation supporting the time spent on this case. Quite a large file as you can imagine."

"Thirty-two thousand dollars in only nine months?" Roberts asked incredulously.

"This case has had extensive opposition," Kendal explained, seeming to stiffen slightly. "We have done a lot of work even before today."

Eyes wide, the commissioner looked down at the piece of paper for a few more minutes.

Mandi had no doubt the bill was fair and accurate. Not only because she had seen the itemized statements every month, but because she knew there was a month or two when Sam seemed to be doing nothing except working for them full-time. At $285 per hour, she found the total number humbling, even aggravating — especially given they were ultimately only fighting to right the wrongs of the original staffing —, but not surprising or suspicious.

"This is astounding," the commissioner said with a shake of his head. "I have no way of knowing if this number is fair without more information. I certainly can't condone the state paying any portion of this. I will need to see supporting documentation before I can determine if there's an amount it's fair for the Division to pay. As such, there's no way I will be able to return a verdict on this case today."

Mandi's jaw dropped. They had never had any expectation the state would pay for anything.

To hold this adoption up yet again? For this? It was all Mandi could do to stay in her seat and keep her mouth shut.

"Your honor," Sam said, clearly caught off guard, "my clients aren't asking and have *never* asked for the state to pay any portion of this. They have already, in fact, paid the majority of it themselves. When they started out, you may recall, the Division hadn't yet turned over the staffing."

"Which it shouldn't have," Payton muttered.

Distracted by the remark, as aggravated as his clients by the mere suggestion this might drag on even one more day, Sam turned to Payton, snapping uncharacteristically, "This isn't a high school classroom, Ms. Gringo, though that comment — particularly given its lack of relevance to the discussion at hand—seems best suited for one."

"You don't—" Payton started angrily, rising threateningly from her chair once again.

"That's enough, counselors," Roberts cut in sardonically. "Let's try to keep our focus on one thing at a time."

Both parties snapped their mouths shut. Payton sat back down.

Commissioner Roberts studied the papers before him a bit longer before shifting his gaze to the far wall, his brow furrowed thoughtfully. Finally, he said, "I believe I have reached a conclusion."

After an additional pause to be certain he had everyone's full attention, he started, "In the matter before this court, case number 2-1-0-5-G-B-1-2-5-7-2, involving the adoption of Baby Girl Reylco, the court confirms its jurisdiction over the subject minor child. In doing so, it finds the following:

"That the sole biological parent of the child has willfully, substantially and continuously abandoned it for a period of at least sixty days prior to the filing of the petition. I can also personally attest to the fact I have never seen said parent in this courtroom, including in the time period well before the petition was filed.

"The biological mother is deceased. The biological father was served in this matter and failed to respond. I entered an Interlocutory Order of Default against him.

"In this matter, there is compliance with the Uniform Child Custody Jurisdiction and Enforcement Act. Also, the Interstate Compact on the Placement of Children and the Indian Welfare Act are inapplicable.

"The petitioners in this case, Justin Rice and Mandi Williams, the current foster family to this little girl, are found to be a suitable family for said child and to have the ability to properly care for, maintain and educate the child.

"Therefore, from this date forward, the child shall, to and for all legal intents and purposes, become and be the child of the petitioners, that the child's name is changed to Jade Reyna Williams-Rice, and that any and all rights which the biological father may have had in and to said child are now terminated."

Commissioner Roberts stopped for a moment to let the words sink in.

Justin had tears in his eyes, while Mandi tried to convince herself that she had heard correctly, that their long fight was finally at a victorious end. Sam beamed at his clients, while Payton started getting her papers together in anticipation of leaving, her face mostly blank.

Rather than immediately dismiss everyone, however, Roberts looked at Mandi and Justin, surprising the occupants of the courtroom by asking, "Do you intend to continue as foster parents?"

Mandi and Justin hesitated, glancing at one another then at their attorney, uncertain how best to respond to the unexpected question. Sam looked as puzzled by the inquiry as they were.

Sensing their apprehension, the commissioner assured them, "The matter before this court has been settled and is final as far as I am concerned, barring any appeal in the next forty-five days. My question is simply one of personal curiosity."

With a remorseful smile, Mandi answered carefully, "Your honor, we might revisit the possibility in the future. We certainly consider our time as foster parents, for all the kids we have had in our care and certainly for Jade, to have been worthwhile despite—" she motioned to the room, "—all of this. However, no, we don't see continuing in that capacity in our immediate future. We have been under tremendous strain for the better part of a year. All we want now is to spend time enjoying our family and friends."

Commissioner Roberts nodded soberly, admitting, "I expected that answer. I can definitely appreciate your point of view."

There were several moments of silence as he studied the notepad he had been writing on throughout the course of the hearing. Everyone waited, forced to be a captive audience until he chose to release them.

"I am looking at this case," he finally started, pausing again to glance at his notes before continuing, "and I see a family who came into this system with an ideal. More than that, unlike many, they made good on that ideal.

"I see individuals who paid cash for medical exams rather than draw on the burdened and inadequate health care plan these children have to rely on; who have paid for formula and food without ever accepting the food stamps this or any previous child was eligible for. I see people who purchased clothes for each child in their care without ever asking for or accepting a clothing voucher. I see a family that has taken all of the kids in their home on various family vacations—St. Louis, Colorado, even Disney World—without any expectation of taxpayer assistance. In this record, I see family portraits that make it obvious whatever children happened to be in their care were always welcomed without reluctance or restriction.

"Then, when that same state agency threatened to take one of the children it had placed with them—not to reunite her with a biological family or to put her with a well-known family friend, but to give her to literal strangers—I see a family who poured all their emotional and financial strength into making certain the system would not terrorize them or this child onto a path that was ill-advised at best, reckless at worst.

"Their fight—where most would have given up and turned away—was incredible for foster parents, but not for a family who operated as if the children in their care were their own, as they obviously did. This kind of love, this kind of loyalty, is what all of the kids stuck in the family court system need. And, with this family, for a time at least, they had it."

Again, Mandi felt tears burn her eyes. They had been defending themselves against attacks for so long now, it felt good being reminded that their role had not always been as the villains.

Roberts looked over at Justin and Mandi. With resignation, he continued, "Yet I see a family we have now likely lost. A state, a country, taxpayers barely able to provide for the needs of these children..."

Payton looked down at the conference table. Jean sat in the back row nodding emphatically.

He shook his head, "It's a shame we have ended up here. I can't help but think how disappointed most of our citizens would be to discover we are alienating families such as this. Not to mention the families, friends, co-workers of this family who have no doubt watched them go through this and are now left thinking there is no way they will ever risk the same level of involvement. This, when there are still too many foster families who take these children in without caring about them, simply for the ability to demand every penny they can from the state."

Shifting his gaze from Mandi and Justin to the rest of the room, he finished, "I have no authority to force it, but I believe it would behoove us all to figure out exactly what went wrong here. I have stacks of documentation as to the care and competency of this family— information that has been available since well before this child entered care. Whether it was a misunderstanding in the beginning escalated by an inability to admit that error or backdoor politics that have nothing to do with the best interests of this individual child, the fact it got to this point is nothing short of reprehensible."

Taking a deep breath, he concluded briskly, "That's all I have to say on the matter. The adoption of Jade Reyna to the Williams-Rice family is granted. Court is dismissed."

From the Author

There were a few individuals who read this manuscript in its infancy and suggested that the last sentence of "Court is dismissed," wasn't enough. They felt the reader would require more closure, some statement of the family's joy or a summary of the consequences or education the antagonists of the story might have received.

I felt it more realistic to leave as is.

First, as a family that has gone through the adoption of a child from the United States, I can tell you that, "Motion granted. Court dismissed," is all the closure any of us need.

Second, because the system remains broken.

In fiction, everything is cleaned up by the last page... victory has been secured, the perpetrators have received enlightenment or been mercilessly punished. In real life, though, victories are achieved but the individuals who abuse the intent of the law for political gain or illegal enforcement of their own personal beliefs are most often left to continue in their attempts to intimidate and terrorize.

It is a disheartening discovery, but a reality we would do well to quickly come to terms with. This is the nature of our democracy. This is, in fact, the nature of any civilization. In a vacuum—whether because of our lack of desire to get involved or our lack of knowledge about our right, our obligation, to get involved—those with duplicitous intentions will happily fill the void. If we are lucky, they are countered tirelessly by those whose motives are just. The amount of luck we rely on in these matters, however, is often nothing short of reckless.

Buddhists have a belief about this moment. That it's important. Not what you did a minute ago or what you are contemplating doing in the next minute, but what's right in front of you—right now—in *this* minute.

The page or screen you are staring at as you read these words? It's real. *Touch it.*

The floor, chair, bed you are sitting on? It's there. *Feel it.*

The breath passing in and out of you? It's giving you life. *Notice it.*

There are approximately 450,000 children in the United States, their average age being nine-years-old, living with nothing more than the reality of this moment. However, instead of the calm and clarity Buddhists find in the here and now, these kids are living in chaos and confusion. They arrive at now with pasts full of abuse and neglect; futures dim and devoid of hope.

For these kids, the objective is simple and singular: survive. They are everything from angry and anti-social to meek and withdrawn. They don't trust others and they don't trust themselves. They live with the paradox of hoping for love, while long ago having stopped believing themselves worthy of it.

These children are the ones whose sole guardianship now lies in the hands of government agencies. These are the children living in foster homes, waiting to see if their parents will get it together so they can come home, or if they will find a family to adopt them, or to simply age out of the system entirely. The ones who are often relying on instinct in place of parental guidance, strangers in the absence of family, movement over the risk of attachment.

You might wonder... *Aren't orphaned, abused and neglected children well provided for within our borders, especially compared to the substandard conditions that exist in other countries?*

Certainly, the children within our borders often have their material needs—shelter, health care, food—met better than their counterparts in other areas of the world. Certainly, if it's a plight a child must endure, they are fortunate to have landed on this country's doorstep. Certainly. There is much we should be proud of, but there is still much to be improved upon. We often think that because we no longer have squalid orphanages, we are done.

We aren't.

We can't be.

The harsh reality of the children who end up in the care of social services is that nobody is coming to America to save them. That citizenship and those material things are of little comfort to a four-year-old who doesn't understand why she doesn't have a mother or a father to love her.

No one can write a story of only a single individual, much like no one can live a life that touches no other. We are all irrefutably intertwined, from the random waitress to our most intimate relationships. Each of us is born to a community. For these kids, though, the community has become their home, their family, their sole source of hope and guidance. Whether we are equipped to effectively reach them directly impacts whether they go on to become productive members of society.

They truly are our children. Maybe we didn't ask for them, but—guess what?—they didn't ask for us either. Unlike some of the leeches our welfare system struggles to support, the youngest in our care have arrived here through little more than someone else's decision to give them life and not much else.

If the system is making it hard for the right people to reach these kids, then we need to figure out how to fix it rather than throw our hands up in frustration and turn away. There is no progress in telling ourselves it is too difficult or too hopeless to attempt; no redemption in saving youngsters from overseas instead, telling ourselves there isn't any point in fighting to make it better here at home.

450,000 American children will tell you they are the point. They don't have the option to walk away. We shouldn't pretend that we do either.

With particular love & gratitude to

Pamela Jean
1943-2010

You were ahead of your time and a classic,

an advocate for the future, a voice of reason about the past,

a tireless ally of the families and children in our county.

Thank you is simply not enough.

www.ingramcontent.com/pod-product-compliance
Lightning Source LLC
LaVergne TN
LVHW091250080426
835510LV00007B/200